"Congress shall make no law . . . abridging the freedom . . . of the press. . . ."
—from the First Amendment to the U. S. Constitution

Interpretations of this principle have caused many clashes between media and government, ranging from the storms of the Pentagon Papers to the Supreme Court battle over whether newsmen must reveal confidential sources.

In the following pages, Professor Stein examines this and other problems relating to the role of the news media in our society. Formerly Chairman of the Department of Journalism and Mass Communications at New York University and currently Chairman of the Department of Journalism at California State University, Professor Stein has authored many books in his field, including **When Presidents Meet the Press**, **Reporting Today** and **Blacks in Communications**.

D0818739

SHAPING THE NEWS:

How the Media Function in Today's World

by

M. L. STEIN

Chairman, Department
of Journalism
California State University
Long Beach, California

WASHINGTON SQUARE PRESS
POCKET BOOKS · NEW YORK

SHAPING THE NEWS

How the Media Function in Today's World

WASHINGTON SQUARE PRESS edition published October, 1974

L

Published by
POCKET BOOKS, a division of Simon & Schuster, Inc.,
630 Fifth Avenue, New York, N.Y.

WASHINGTON SQUARE PRESS editions are distributed
in the U.S. by Simon & Schuster, Inc., 630 Fifth Avenue,
New York, N.Y. 10020, and in Canada by Simon & Schuster of Canada, Ltd., Markham, Ontario, Canada.

1254

Contents

Shaping

the

News:

How the Media Function
in Today's World

CHAPTER ONE

Free Country—Free Press

THE PRESS IS having its problems these days. Reporters have been tossed in jail for refusing to name sources of information. The last two presidents have fought with newspapers and broadcasters over their coverage of the Vietnam war, the Watergate scandal, the cost of living, and other issues. Many editors are convinced that President Richard Nixon and members of his administration launched a calculated program to destroy the credibility of the press in the public mind. But even without such encouragement, large numbers of readers view the mass media with suspicion, if not fear. One reason for this is that the newspapers and television frequently bear bad news, and few people like bad news. There is also the feeling among some persons that the media have an unwholesome influence on lifestyles, morals, and the crime rate.

It is unlikely that the Founding Fathers would be much surprised by all this. They took with them to the New World the memory of press censorship and repression in England. In 1275, even before the invention of the printing press, the British parliament adopted the De Scandalis Magnatum law which made it a crime to "tell or publish any false news or tales whereby discord or occasion of discord or slander may grow." When the printing press was developed in 1475 by William Caxton, the English rulers knew they had a potential troublemaker on their hands and acted accordingly. In the first half of the sixteenth century, King Henry VIII issued a list of forbidden books and gave orders that printers must be licensed. Violators frequently lost their heads to the royal executioner after being charged with treason at a secret hearing. The proceedings produced the term "Star Chamber Court," an expression still used to describe official meetings held behind closed doors. The name derived from the stars painted on the ceiling of the English courtroom.

Colonial America under the British Crown was scarcely more hospitable to the press. Under pain of swift punishment, no paper could be printed without a license. A 1689 decree declared that persons who violated the edict would be "accounted enemies to Their Majesties' present government and be proceeded against as such with uttermost severity." The last thing the king's representatives wanted was new ideas which could be distributed in printed form. The same thought prevails today in many nations where the press is under strict control and censorship.

But ideas seek outlets and the situation in New England was no exception. The first newspaper in the colonies was started by Benjamin Harris, who was not one of journalism's more notable practitioners. Before coming to America he had published a London newspaper known chiefly for its bigoted attacks against Catholics and Quakers. After serving nine months in prison for offenses against the Crown, he emigrated to Boston, where he opened the London Coffee House in 1690. In that same year, he printed his one and only edition of a tiny newspaper called *Publick Occurrences Both Forreign and Domestick*. It lasted one day.

Two of its stories infuriated the Mather family, who ruled the Massachusetts Bay Colony with an iron grip. One concerned Mohawk Indian mistreatment of prisoners seized during the border fighting between Canada and the colonies. Officially, the Mohawks were considered friendly to the colonists and the Mathers didn't want to offend them. Harris did just that, referring to them as "miserable savages."

The other item cast a moral slur upon the King of France which, the Mathers reasoned, would be embarrassing to the English monarch. Harris also made one other error in judgment: he had neglected to take out a license to publish. The sheet was quickly suppressed and the remaining copies destroyed.

The lesson was not lost on John Campbell, a Boston postmaster, who was the second colonial to take a shot at journalism. His Boston *News-Letter,* which first appeared on April 24, 1704, carried this significant note under the logotype: "Published by Authority." Campbell had had no publishing experience, but the post office was the town's gathering place and gossip mill. Besides, he had a built-in delivery system in the postboys who regularly carried the mail. In a few years, however, Campbell lost interest in the paper and it passed into other hands.

Campbell had bowed to authority by steering away from controversial items. However, some of his successors in the newspaper business were not that subservient, thereby establishing a tradition of independence that continues to this day. One of the early mavericks was James Franklin, who, with his brother, Ben, established the *New England Courant,* a lively, irreverent broadside that jabbed the ruling powers with unmistakable relish. In one issue, the editor twitted the colonial governor for his seeming reluctance to go after pirates who were harassing shipping off the coast. The governor reacted by throwing James in jail. While he was behind bars, the single-sheet paper was taken over by Ben, who signed his articles "Silence Dogood." When James was freed a month later he again took up the cudgel against local magistrates while Cotton Mather, the clan leader, fumed. In one issue, James Franklin wrote: "There are many persons who seem to be more than ordinary religious, but yet are on several accounts worse, by far, than those who pretend to no religion at all."

By this time the *Courant* had become an organ for dissident elements in the colony, several of whom poked fun at the authorities in letters to the editors above such pen names as Timothy Turnstone, Ichabod Henroost, and Abigail Afterwit. Friends of the newspaper persuaded James to let Ben become the nominal editor as a means of keeping the older brother out of hot water. The scheme worked for a while, but Ben took his job too seriously to suit James, who become jealous of the reputation his former apprentice was rapidly acquiring. In the end, they quarreled and Ben left to found his own newspaper in Philadelphia, the *Pennsylvania Gazette,* which became one of the outstanding journals in the colonies. He later, of course, went on to fame in government and diplomacy, but it was his journalistic talent that first made him a public figure.

Meanwhile, the printing trade continued to expand along the eastern shore. In the 1730s, newspapers started up in New York, Philadelphia, Boston, Newport, and Charleston, and also in a few smaller communities. Most publishers, remembering what happened to Harris, were careful not to arouse the wrath of the king's men. The editor-printers included a number of individuals who were more interested in making money than in leading revolutionary causes. In addition to putting out a newspaper, some publishers carried on a brisk trade in soap, candles, and stationery which they advertised in their sheets. Other advertisements for patent medicines strayed so far from the truth that one wonders how they convinced anyone—even in that day. One such ad proclaimed that a particular medication could cure "Cholick, Dry Belly-Ache, Consumption, Smallpox, Gravel, Melancholy," as well as "Loss of Limbs."

News content varied with the publisher's enterprise and affluence. Most newspapers made a regular practice of extracting stories from the London journals on such topics as English politics, European wars, court trials, and social chitchat. Local news usually consisted of ship arrivals, obituaries, sermons, political appoint-

DEPARTMENT OF DEFENSE

A correspondent for the *New York Herald Tribune* pauses at a press camp site, during a lull in the fighting, near a Civil War battle front. The horse and wagon (right) were the only satisfactory means of following the action.

ments, the weather, Indian attacks on settlers, piracies, court cases, and crimes. Essentially, readers then were interested in the same things as today's readers. The colonials, however, did not receive the news in quite the same form as it is now presented. Early-day editors made little distinction between news and personal opinion, frequently mingling the two. The objective style of journalism in today's newspapers would not come for about 150 years. A personal kind of writing continued in American newspapers through the Civil War and into the late nineteenth century, which saw the birth of mass circulation dailies. The use of editorials and columnists to advance personal opinion is a relatively new development in American journalism. Although it is true that pure objectivity may be hard to find in any newspaper, nevertheless, it is the standard by which reporters write today.

One newspaper got too personal in 1733 for the English governor of New York, a tyrant named William Cosby. The paper was owned and edited by John Peter Zenger, an obscure German immigrant, who was destined to become a symbol of press freedom in the United States. An unsophisticated man, Zenger was only a so-so printer and an even worse writer. His newspaper, the New York *Weekly Journal,* was unimpressive, even by colonial standards of journalism. It was a tiny, four-page sheet with blurry type and drab makeup. Zenger was able to keep the paper afloat by doing odd-job printing on the side.

Zenger's name might have passed unnoticed into history along with scores of other colonial printers, but for a raw power play by Cosby. The governor dismissed Chief Justice Lewis Morris, one of the colony's most respected figures, and replaced him with the young son of a personal crony. The action enraged a political group which had long opposed Cosby and had lent their support to the *Weekly Journal* as a means of making their opposition known. Justice Morris' ouster was quickly followed by a *Journal* article which read in part: "We see men's deeds destroyed, judges arbitrarily displaced, new courts erected without the consent of the legislature, by which, it seems to me, trials by juries are taken away when a governor pleases; men of known estates denied their votes, contrary to the received practice, the best expositor of any law. Who is there in that province that can call anything his own or enjoy any liberty longer than those in the administration will condescend to let them do it . . . ?"

Cosby exploded, ordering the king's soldiers to burn every copy of the *Journal* they could find. Still, the newspaper continued its weekly criticisms of Cosby and his henchmen with withering editorials or slyly humorous pokes. An opposition newspaper, the *Gazette,* took the governor's side, suggesting in one issue that the English language ought to be changed to make Zenger a synonym for liar.

At Cosby's instructions, the chief justice tried several times to get the grand jury to indict Zenger for "seditious libel," a criminal offense, but without success. Finally, Cosby was forced to issue his own warrant for the printer's arrest, thereby setting the stage for one of the most famous trials in American history.

Pale and drawn after spending almost nine months in prison, John Zenger came to trial on August 4, 1735. It was a steaming hot day but the courtroom was packed, mostly with Zenger's admirers. He was defended by an eighty-year-old Philadelphia lawyer, Andrew Hamilton, who was a friend of Benjamin Franklin.

From a legal standpoint, Hamilton had a pitifully weak case. The anti-Cosby articles *had been* published and they *did,* according to English law, constitute criminal libel. But the old man was a shrewd attorney and he knew the temper of the times. Instead of denying the formal charge, he concentrated on the *truth* of the *Journal*'s charges against Cosby and company.

Standing erect before the jurors, he declared: "The question before the court and you, gentlemen of the jury, is not of small or private concern. It is not the cause of a poor printer, nor of New York alone, which you are trying. No! It may, in its consequences, affect every freeman that lives under a British government on the main of America. It is the best cause; it is the cause of liberty; and I make no doubt but your upright conduct this day will not only entitle you to the love and esteem of your fellow citizens, but every man who prefers freedom to a life of slavery will bless you and honor you as men who have baffled the attempts of tyranny; and by an impartial and uncorrupt verdict have laid a noble foundation for securing to ourselves, our posterity, and our neighbors that to which nature and the laws of our country have given us a right— the liberty—both of exposing and opposing arbitrary power in those parts of the world at least, by speaking and writing truth."

The jury found Zenger not guilty and he was lifted to the shoulders of the joyous spectators who swarmed around him. It mattered little that the Cosby articles probably had been written by others. It was Zenger who had been arrested, served time in prison, and was acquitted in a trial that had all New York buzzing. He was the hero of the day and bonfires were lit in his honor that night. The victory gave courage to every editor, writer, or printer who wanted the freedom to say what he pleased without fear of punishment. Zenger's name is still invoked by journalists as a symbol for press freedom. The University of Arizona each year bestows the "John Peter Zenger Award" for courageous reporting. The Westchester County (N.Y.) chapter of Sigma Delta Chi, the professional journalistic society, is named in Zenger's honor.

Zenger's triumph did not lead to immediate press freedom in the colonies. This would not come until after America won its independence from Britain. English governors and magistrates continued to harass publishers, closing their shops, destroying their papers, and casting them behind bars when they offended authority. Isaiah Thomas, editor of the *Massachusetts Spy,* for example, was hounded out of Boston by the administration, which took away his advertising, denied him shipping information, and otherwise made his life miserable. Later, after setting up an underground paper in Worcester, he became America's first war correspondent by reporting the Battle of Lexington from the best possible vantage point—that of a member of the colonial militia.

Other publishers, fired up by the Zenger verdict, grew bolder as the independence movement grew in the colonies. The Stamp Act of 1765 was a landmark in the struggle for a free press. It so hurt newspapers that even moderate and nonpolitical editors joined in denouncing the British for this taxation without representation. The act, which was to help the English pay for their war against France, required that all official documents, books, and newspapers carry an official stamp for which some publishers had to pay 50 percent of the paper's purchase price. For the weaker journals this meant going out of business, since the proprietors could not afford the tax. Those newspapers which purchased the stamp were threatened with boycotts and, in some instances, hotheaded mobs.

The Stamp Act was repealed a year later, thanks largely to the unrelenting assaults on it by colonial newspapers. Benjamin Franklin, then in London as a representative of the Pennsylvania Colony, was a potent factor in persuading the British king to revoke the law.

By the time the colonies had achieved their independence from Britain, the concept of a free press was firmly in the minds of the Founding Fathers. Thomas Jefferson felt strongly that the Constitution should clearly guarantee press freedom. In 1787, he stated: "The basis of our government being the opinion of the people, the very first object should be to keep that right; and were it left to me to decide whether we should have a government without newspapers or newspapers without government, I should not hesitate a moment to prefer the latter. But I should mean that every man should receive those papers and be capable of reading them."

Alexander Hamilton had a different view, stirring a debate which, in one form or another, is still going on today. Writing in *The Federalist,* Hamilton said: ". . . What is liberty of the press? Who can give it any definition which would not leave the utmost latitude for evasion? I hold it to be impracticable; and from this I infer that its security, whatever fine declarations may be inserted in any constitution respecting it, must altogether depend on public opinion, and on the general spirit of the people and of the government. And here, after all, as is intimated upon another occasion, must we seek for the only solid basis of all our rights."

Jefferson and other guarantee advocates prevailed. Freedom of the press was written into the First Amendment to the Constitution, which holds that: "Congress shall make no law respecting an establishment of religion, or prohibiting the free exercise thereof; or abridging the freedom of speech or of the press; or the right of the people to assemble and to petition the Government for redress of grievances."

Plain as these words are, the question of *how* free the press should be is still a matter of debate. It is generally recognized that the First Amendment does not exempt newspapers from the laws of libel. The Constitutional guarantee forbids prior restraint, which is understood to mean that news shall not be subjected to government censorship before it is printed. But newspapers (as well as other print media) publish at their peril. If a news item is damaging to someone's character or reputation he is entitled to sue the publication under state law and collect damages if he wins.

In recent years, however, the issue of precensorship of the news media has arisen, with the First Amendment itself called into question. In a later chapter we shall discuss the Pentagon Papers case, the Watergate scandal, and other events in which the press's traditional claim to absolute freedom has been challenged by government officials. As this is written, publishers are dismayed by a United States Supreme Court decision upholding a Pittsburgh ordinance prohibiting newspapers from printing sex-designated employment advertisements. According to the ruling, newspapers can no longer carry "Help Wanted—Male" or "Help Wanted—Female." Newspaper executives generally agreed with Justice Potter Stewart, who dissented from the majority opinion, posing this question: "If government can dictate the layout of a newspaper's classified advertising pages today, what is there to prevent it from dictating the layout of the news pages tomorrow?"

At the same time, the high court, in another case, handed down guidelines on obscenity that enabled local communities to ban books, magazines, plays, and movies considered offensive to local standards of taste, even if they might be acceptable elsewhere. The decision could have the effect of prior censorship if editors withhold certain pictures or articles from their publications or "clean them up" before printing. The tone of the ruling was felt immediately in some communities where shops and theaters dealing in pornographic literature and films closed down.

The First Amendment guarantee hit its first snag in 1798 with the passage of the Alien and Sedition Acts, whose principal purpose was to deport undesirable aliens. However, the Federalist Congress, which adopted the laws, was well aware that several editors of Republican newspapers opposed to the Federalists were European refugees. One act prescribed a prison sentence and fine for anyone convicted of writing, printing, or uttering "false, scandalous and malicious" statements against the government or Congress with the intention of ridiculing or holding them up to contempt. Twenty-five arrests were made under the law, which many editors charged was a gag on the press. The act's first victim was John D. Burk, a hard-hitting editor for *The New York Times,* who was indicted for libeling President John Adams. Burk fled to avoid arrest and was later killed in a duel in Virginia.

The government also went after other newspapers. A New York Republican paper, *The Argus,* ran a story saying that Alexander Hamilton, then out of office but still a weighty political figure, intended to buy *The Argus* and then shut it down. Hamilton demanded prosecution and marshals arrested the widow of the paper's late owner and one of her printers. The case against the widow was dropped, but the printer, who earned eight dollars a week, was fined one hundred dollars and sentenced to four months in jail. In Boston, the prime federal target was the *Independent Chronicle,* whose editor, Thomas Adams, had chided the Massachusetts legislature for not protesting the Alien and Sedition Acts. Because of illness, Thomas was not prosecuted, but the government indicted his brother, Abijah, the bookkeeper, who was in good health. He was convicted, sent to jail for thirty days and forced to pay bail for good behavior in the future. James T. Callender, an English refugee, was fined two hundred dollars and sentenced to nine months in prison for a piece in the Richmond *Examiner* heaping scorn on President Adams.

The Alien and Sedition Acts died with the Federalist Congress. Upon becoming President, Thomas Jefferson pardoned everyone convicted under the laws, which were branded unconstitutional by the new Congress. Those who had been fined under the acts were reimbursed with interest.

Although no legislation resembling the Alien and Sedition Acts has since been adopted, the press in the United States has not escaped official harassment and attempts at control. Some states have attempted to impose special taxes on newspaper advertising and circulation. One state legislator even proposed that newsmen be licensed, a practice common in certain foreign countries. In the past few years, many editors and reporters felt that the White House had been trying to muzzle both printed and broadcast media through verbal attacks by former Vice-President Spiro T. Agnew and by forcing reporters to reveal confidential sources of information.

But an adversary relationship between the press and government always has existed in this country. Many persons on both sides regard it as a healthy condition. George Washington fumed over journalistic reports that he had illegally taken over Virginia property belonging to his old friend, Lord Fairfax. He also was outraged over attacks on his policies by several newspapers, notably the *National Gazette,* published by Philip Freneau, the "Poet of the American Revolution." When opposition journals became too vitriolic for his taste, Washington simply refused to read them, a decision that was to be taken almost two hundred years later by President John F. Kennedy in connection with the *New York Herald Tribune.*

John Adams and succeeding presidents sought to offset newspaper criticism by establishing their own papers which hewed to the government line and retaliated against its detractors. Thomas Jefferson persuaded Samuel Harrison Smith to move his *National*

Intelligencer from Philadelphia to Washington, where it became the mouthpiece for Jefferson's administration. The party press died out in the nineteenth century, but vestiges survive in the form of editorial endorsements of presidential and other political candidates by newspapers and magazines.

The reason for press-government feuding is quite simple. The reporter's job is to get the news. The government, one of the main news sources, frequently is reluctant to tell everything it knows. The news media argue that a well-informed electorate is essential to a democratic system. The government agrees in principle, but says there are times when the public should not know everything immediately—as in the case of reports which might jeopardize our national security. The news people say they are willing to make an exception for national security, but charge that government often conceals information for reasons having nothing to do with security—information to which citizens are entitled access.

This issue and others will be explored in this book. But first, let's find out more about the mass media and how they work.

CHAPTER TWO

How News Gets Around

NEWS IS ONE of the most vital products we consume. It is also one of the most perishable. The worker who contributes to the making of a car, bridge, house, or even a pair of shoes knows his effort has produced something that will endure—perhaps beyond his lifetime. Not so with the news worker. The story on which he labored so hard and which he wrote so eloquently will be on its way to the recycling machine a day later —if it's not used to wrap fish. By then he is gathering facts for his next story. By the same token, who can remember the words of a television or radio news announcer twenty-four hours afterward?

The fleeting quality of news helps in explaining how it is obtained, written, edited, printed, and distributed. This process continues twenty-four hours a day to satisfy a worldwide demand for fresh information. On the basis of the news we get, we vote, buy, sell, make or change plans, carry an umbrella to work, attend the theater, go to a meeting, or write a letter to the mayor. Thus, the newspaper at the breakfast table and the eleven o'clock TV news shows are part of our lives. We want to know what's going on. The news media tell us.

To supply news, a huge army of people work around the clock throughout the world. United Press International, a globe-circling press agency, operates on the slogan, "A Deadline Every Minute." This means

AP

AP staffer John Paul Filo talks with U.S. Coast Guardsmen in Cape Girardeau, Missouri, at the flooding Mississippi River on May 1, 1973.

that somewhere in the world one or more of its clients is going to press or on the air with news.

The key word is "deadline." News is gathered under deadline pressure. The reporter is always aware that his story must be in the hands of his editor by a rigidly prescribed time. The editor, in turn, knows that the edited copy must be in the print shop by a specific time if it is to get into the paper. Newsmen work by the clock. As the newspapers roll off the press, circulation trucks are waiting to haul them to various parts of the city and to trains and planes that will take them to more distant points. The same pressure applies to broadcasting. A television news crew must have its film and tape at the studio by a certain time if the spot is to be aired that evening. Even magazines have to meet deadlines, although not as tight ones.

Does deadline pressure affect the quality and accuracy of the news? Of course. Reporters working at great speed in gathering and writing news stories cannot always tie up loose ends, furnish sufficient background for total comprehension, or give both sides of an issue. And inaccuracies may crop up. Newsmen and women often obtain information under less than ideal conditions—at the frenzied scene of an accident or above the shouts of a mob. The most conscientious of reporters is liable to miss the correct spelling of a name or get an address wrong. Also, news sources don't always tell the truth and often there isn't time to verify given statements.

But remember, editors and reporters are meeting the public demand for news shortly after events happen. They are dealing in instant history. The news in perspective, the background details, and so forth can be handled by the columnists, in editorials and in long interpretive or "think" pieces in the Sunday paper. Daily newspapers also carry "sidebars," or features which give more depth and illumination to the main story. As for accuracy, studies have shown that newspapers and wire services have a high batting average on this score considering the hectic pace at which news is produced. But this does not give the news media a blanket excuse to commit errors. It is possible to double-check facts even on a fast-breaking story and reporters fail their obligation when they don't do so. In fact, inaccuracies result as much from careless news people as from the necessity for speedy coverage. However, the reporter who is consistently inaccurate will not last long with a news organization. Editors know that when readers lose confidence in a newspaper its future is bleak.

A clearer picture of the news process may emerge from a look at the way different news media work.

NEWSDAY

The press room at *Newsday*, a Long Island newspaper

The Daily Newspaper

Someone who derived his notion of newspaper practice exclusively from movies, TV dramas and popular literature would be in for a surprise if he walked into a city room, where local news is written and edited. He wouldn't hear anyone shouting, "Stop the presses!" or see any reporters wearing press cards in their hatbands or editors gulping from a whiskey bottle after yelling on the telephone. He *would* witness some hurried activity, especially near deadline time, and the simultaneous clattering of twenty or thirty typewriters and teletype machines would indicate that he was not in the sedate offices of a bank. But if he looked closely, he would notice that the stepped-up action was controlled, that everyone from the managing editor to the copy boys knew his job and was doing it with a minimum of lost motion. Copy would be flowing smoothly from the reporters' desks to the city editor. From there it would move to the copy desk, where headlines would be written, and then to the composing room, where it would be set in type. Once in a while someone might call out for a copy boy but voices generally would be at a moderate level.

The newsroom structure on a daily newspaper is quite standard. However, the number of editors, reporters, copy readers, and the like varies widely with the size of the paper. *The New York Times* has more than four hundred editorial employees, seventy-six in financial writing alone. A small daily in Wisconsin may have a reporting staff of six, who handle any kind of story.

Local news is the responsibility of the city or metropolitan editor. He assigns reporters to cover city hall, the police, the courts, various commissions, and suburban communities. He also must have reporters and photographers on hand to send out on spot news stories such as fires, accidents, and demonstrations. These men and women are called general assignment report-

Controlled action in the newsroom of *Newsday,* a Long Island newspaper

The copy desk (foreground) and news desk (background) of *The Record* in Hackensack, New Jersey

WASHINGTON POST

Washington Post photographer Matthew Lewis

ers. In the course of a single day they may cover and write stories ranging from an interview with the ambassador from Nigeria to a nursing home fire. The reporters assigned to city hall, police headquarters, etc., are called "beat" men (or women). Instead of working out of the city room like the general assignment staffers, their desks are in the press room at police headquarters, the criminal courts building, or city hall. These specialists are also, in a sense, editors. They are the eyes and ears of the city editor and often make judgments on what and what not to cover on their beats. A police reporter, for example, may decide that a certain burglary is too trivial to bother with and does not tell his city desk about it.

Contrary to another popular myth, reporters do not wander the streets looking for news. Stories are assigned by the editor who knows where his staff members are at all times. A reporter may stumble upon a news item but this is the exception rather than the rule. The editors are in a far better position to know where news is happening. Their sources of information include news releases from public relations representatives, the wire services (more about them later), their beat men, tips from known or unknown persons, and the official notices of meetings, press conferences, etc., that are normally made available to the news media by various agencies.

In addition to the general assignment and beat reporters, the larger newspapers have other specialists who work out of the newsroom but who more or less create their own assignments simply because they are more familiar with sources of information in their fields than anyone else, including editors. These men and women are experts in reporting on science, medicine, politics, environment, crime, urban affairs, theater, finance, labor, and other areas. From the ranks of these journalists often come the investigative reporters, who make headlines with sensational disclosures about corruption, dirty politics, or international conspiracies. One learns quickly in the news business that all news

NEWSDAY

Copy for the *Newsday* Sunday package

isn't announced. To bring it before the public occasionally requires long and hard digging beneath the surface of events. The treatment of the Watergate scandal is a recent example of investigative journalism at its best.

On the larger dailies, news of sports, women's activities, the performing arts, and finance is handled in separate sections, usually with their own editors. Sports writers, for example, take their assignments from the sports editor and submit their copy to him rather than the city editor. These sectional editors are generally given wide latitude in deciding what to cover but, like the editors in the general news departments, they are under the jurisdiction of the managing editor. The latter determines how much space will be devoted to news, as opposed to advertising, columns, and editorials, and where stories will appear in the paper. He may rule that an airplane hijacking is more significant than a local bond issue and make it the "lead" story with a banner headline. The city editor and the other editors are informed at the start of the working day how much space they will have for their departments. Sometimes, however, a particular editor may successfully appeal the order, citing a particular story as being of overwhelming importance. Usually, about half of a newspaper's content is advertising.

The telegraph or wire editor also competes for space with the local or regional news editors. He and his assistants screen and edit the thousands of words that come over the leased wires of the Associated Press or United Press International, the two major wire services which cover the earth. Most newspapers use only a fraction of the outpouring of state, national, and international news that is fed them on the teleprinter machines from bureaus around the world. Metropolitan dailies like *The New York Times,* the *Washington Post,* the *St. Louis Post-Dispatch,* and the *Chicago Tribune* feature the biggest chunk of national and foreign news. Small newspapers normally run only major items from abroad on the theory that their readers are more interested in hometown events. To the editor of a small Kansas daily, local wheat production or even the burglary of the five-and-dime store may take precedence over a two-thousand-word AP story on the European Common Market. Press critics, including foreigners, have charged that American newspapers are too provincial in their selection of news, with the result that their readers are uninformed about international affairs. There is some truth to this statement, since most U.S. newspapers receive their news about the outside world from AP or UPI. The wire services will be discussed later in more detail.

News copy is written by reporters and read by various editors for accuracy, style, taste, possible libel, grammar, spelling, and punctuation. If a deadline is near, the story is written in "short takes," that is, two or three paragraphs at a time, which are rushed up to the city editor, who scans them quickly for errors and moves them along to the managing editor or his assistants. They also check the content and then forward the story to the copy desk. Here, copy editors, sitting around a horseshoe-shaped desk, give the item a further check for grammar and style before writing a headline for it. The headline is a brief, present-tense summary of the story designed to attract reader attention. The best of the copy editors are adept at wording the nub of a fifteen-hundred-word story in two or three short lines. But sometimes the head does not accurately reflect the body of the story, leading to sensational distortions. Many readers who complain about biased or overplayed news are actually referring to the headline. The story itself may be a sober, objective account of a speech, rally, or other event. In one case, a New York afternoon paper ran a screaming banner headline that indicated a full-scale war was about to erupt in the Middle East. A reading of the wire service story made it quite clear that neither Israel nor the Arab states were at that stage.

A reader may wonder if he is getting *all* the facts in a story. The answer: probably not. The First Amendment to the Constitution bars government censorship of news, but it says nothing about internal censorship on newspapers, a commonplace practice. In gathering news and writing it, reporters must often omit certain facts to save space, avoid libel, or conform to good taste. As professionals, newsmen and women are expected to make judgments about what to include and not to include in a story. They take more notes than they will actually use in writing the article. When he goes over his notes before and during the writing, a reporter automatically eliminates material which is of lesser importance or which may be impossible to confirm at the time. Many of the gorier details are kept out of police stories, despite the notion of some people that newspapers "play up" crime news. Also, newsmen may withhold certain facts in a crime story at the request of police, who contend their disclosure would jeopardize an investigation. Such material might consist of clues found at the scene or the name of a suspect still at large.

The news story undergoes further censorship at the hands of the city editor and the copy reader. If an editor thinks the article is too long or padded, he will pencil out part of it. If he believes a certain quotation or assertion contains the risk of character defamation (libel), he will remove that, too. Newspapers are not anxious to invite lawsuits. It is possible that a whole story will be killed for one reason or another. The publisher, who normally does not interfere in newsroom operations, may exercise his authority at times and ban a story or a specific reference. *The Kansas City Star* writers were once forbidden to use the word "snake" in their stories on the premise that it would offend breakfast readers. The late William Randolph Hearst, one of the nation's press lords, once forbade (for reasons that are obscure) any mention of Stanford University in the columns of any of his chain of newspapers. The *Christian Science Monitor* carries no crime news, and one newspaper, for which the author worked, rejected any divorce items.

The straight news story is written in a traditional style known as the "inverted pyramid." The most important element goes in the lead or first paragraph, regardless of when it occurred in the sequence of events. Facts are then presented in a descending order of value, with the least important details at the end. Thus, if a reader is in a hurry, he can get a reasonably good picture of what's happening in the world by glancing at the headline and reading the first two or three paragraphs of stories. Note how the following account is organized to give the reader the salient facts in the first few paragraphs:

Wellington, New Zealand—France today triggered the first nuclear explosion in its much-protested 1973 test series with a shot high above its proving grounds in the South Pacific.

The device was triggered from a sausage-shaped balloon at 2:00 P.M. yesterday (New York time) above Mururoa Atoll, 720 miles southeast of Tahiti.

A New Zealand Defense Ministry spokesman said the weather at the atoll was perfect for the shot. Radio Australia said the blast was reported by the New Zealand frigate *Otago,* which was stationed about twenty miles upwind of the explosion, well inside the seventy-two-mile danger zone the French proclaimed around the test site. The *Otago* was manned by a volunteer crew. Also aboard was Fraser Colman, minister for mines and immigration, as an official representative of the government. The crew was allowed on deck minutes after the blast, and saw a gigantic pillar of smoke climbing into the sky, the radio report said.

New Zealand Prime Minister, Norman E. Kirk, in a statement issued early this morning, ordered a strong protest to be conveyed to the French government through the New Zealand Embassy in Paris. He said news of the test would be greeted with profound dismay in New Zealand and many other countries.

The French Defense Ministry, which had declined even to say when the test would be made, said it would have no comment on reports that it had taken place. "We have no comment and do not expect to have any," a ministry spokesman said.

In an interview with the Sydney (Australia) commercial broadcasting station shortly before the test, Colman was asked about reports of a U.S. ship in the vicinity of the French test area.

"Yes, we have sighted it," he replied. "She was within three or four miles of the *Otago* this afternoon. Earlier in the day, a helicopter with the markings of the United States Navy flew by the frigate *Otago* but at no time has the ship or the helicopter endeavored to contact *Otago.*"

The San Francisco-registered protest yacht *Fri* was boarded by French sailors three days ago and towed out of the danger zone.

France ignored a stream of world protests against the blast, the thirty-fourth nuclear explosion since France began testing in the area in 1966, and also defied a World Court order handed down June 23 that it discontinue nuclear tests in the Pacific.

A French Foreign Ministry white paper issued last month said that as of January 1, 1972, France had exploded thirty nuclear devices in the atmosphere.

In Papeete, Tahiti, yesterday, two Tahitian lawmakers said they sent French President Georges Pompidou a telegram warning that they would seek independence for French Polynesia . . .

—*Newsday*

Although still relying on the basic inverted pyramid form, a number of newspapers are developing new styles of news presentation. This is partly because television and radio have snatched away the newspaper's historic claim to being first with the news. TV and radio stations can broadcast spot news much faster than newspapers can make the mechanical changes necessary to put an extra into the streets. In fact, the extra has all but disappeared from American journalism.

To combat the electronic media's advantage in transmitting breaking news to the public, newspapers have recently begun to concentrate on a kind of reporting that TV does infrequently and not very well. It is reporting in depth—putting the news into clearer focus by providing interpretation and background on complicated matters such as Watergate, the Common Market, arms limitation agreements, poverty, the cost of living, unemployment, and other social, economic, and political matters. Reporters are being assigned to write long articles or a series of articles on issues of the day. Television, of course, offers its "specials" and documentaries, but not on a daily or even weekly basis. Smaller dailies cannot compete with *The New York Times* and the *Washington Post* in this kind of staff reporting, but they can obtain similar pieces from the wire services to which they subscribe. A seven-thousand-circulation daily in Oregon may, if it desires, run a five-thousand-word article by a nationally recognized AP or UPI expert on science, European politics, or education.

These in-depth stories take various forms, ranging from a question and answer approach to one in which the writer becomes closely involved with the lives of his subjects. An example of the former might deal with a presidential economic plan to curb rising prices. The questions would be those likely to be asked by any consumer, such as whether a price freeze will produce food shortages. The answers are supplied by the newspaper's specialist on economic affairs.

The personally involved writing has come to be known as the "New Journalism" and is not popular among all editors. Nonetheless, New Journalism practitioners such as Gay Talese, Tom Wolfe, Hunter Thompson, Gail Sheehy, and Pete Hamill have gained popularity among many newspaper and magazine readers. Their feature style, combined with an intimate closeup of their subjects, is apparently in tune with journalism in the 1970s—and perhaps beyond. Candid treatment of drugs, sex, abortion, prostitution, street people, poverty, and so forth is characteristic of the New Journalism, along with an unconventional format. Tom Wolfe's book, *The Electric Kool-Aid Acid Test,* is a prime example of the method.

It might be a good idea here to examine the men and women in journalism today, as well as what they write and how. Again we must explode a few cherished myths. The long-held stereotype of the newspaperman is that of a tough-talking, shifty-eyed character who isn't too particular about how he gets the story. He usually has a cigarette dangling from his lips, a press card in his hat, and, if he is not an alcoholic, he is leaning in that direction. To complete the portrait, he is semi-educated, a drifter by choice, a seedy dresser, and usually broke.

Journalism, like any other business or profession, has its unsavory members, but the above stereotype is gone with the Jazz Age and Prohibition—if it ever existed to any great extent. Today's journalism has no room for badly educated reporters who try to bully the news out of anyone. Newspapermen and women are mostly college graduates (including many with advanced degrees), idealistic, well-dressed, civil, ethical, and have stable employment records. Editors, station managers, and others who hire for the media do not have to settle for unqualified applicants. There are so many highly qualified, personable candidates for jobs that competition alone rules out the admission of many bad apples into the field. More than fifty thousand students are majoring in journalism at U.S. colleges and universities.

Journalists today are generally well educated, better informed than the average individual, and quite a number have a crusading streak. They sincerely want to make the world a better place and many chose their profession because of the opportunities it provides for helping to improve society. Many staffers on newspapers, magazines, and broadcast outlets are young people in their twenties and thirties. A number of women reporters are married, some have children, and they handle all kinds of stories, not merely "women's news." In recent years, the number of blacks and other minority group members has increased in the news media, although they still lag well behind whites in media employment.

Television Journalism

Television is the glamor boy of the news business. TV news announcers quickly become celebrities. Surveys have indicated that video news has taken over from newspapers as the main information source for many people. Some viewers who don't believe what they read put their absolute trust in the six o'clock news. Besides, television can do a number of things that newspapers cannot, such as show action pictures of fires, riots, battles, political conventions, Senate hearings, and football games. In addition, the news on the screen is concise, not too complicated, and the

NBC

TV newsmen John Chancellor (left) and David Brinkley cover
the 1972 Republican Convention in Miami Beach.

men and women who deliver it are usually physically
attractive.

All in all, it's a package that's hard to beat. Television is indeed an exciting news medium. Some of its
coverage is superlative and no one questions that it is
capable reportage that is beyond the possibilities of
print journalism. But glamor has its drawbacks. Television is primarily an entertainment industry in which
news takes second or third place. Add up all the broadcasting hours on your TV set and then count the number of minutes devoted to news. In comparison to the
overall content, the news shows take up very little
time. There is usually a six o'clock half-hour or hour-long news presentation and another at 10:00 or 11:00
P.M. TV's habit is to skim the news highlights and to
emphasize events that produce the most striking visual
effects. Some significant news never gets reported at
all on television because editors cannot transform a

council meeting or interview into something exciting enough for the home screens. Great issues may be debated in Congress, but debates are not usually the stuff of which TV news programs are made. Newspapers, of course, present a more complete package, carrying more news than the two daily TV shows combined.

Gathering news for television involves many of the same principles used by newspaper reporters. In fact, a number of TV newsmen come from the ranks of daily newspapers. There are certain essential differences, however. TV writers, reporters, and editors think in terms of visual impact and stories are generally selected for that reason. The choice is made by an assignment editor whose function parallels that of a city editor on a newspaper. Twelve hours before air-time the assignment editor arrives at his office, having already read the morning newspapers. He checks the calendar to determine what's happening in the city that day and also scans press releases that have piled up on his desk. On large TV stations an assignment editor is on duty twenty-four hours a day.

A little later the news crews come in. Here is where the city editor and the assignment editor face quite dif-

NBC

NBC News Election Night coverage

ferent problems. It's a simple matter to send a newspaper reporter and cameraman to the scene of a story. They can go by car or public transportation. Covering an assignment for a TV news show is literally a production. Camera crewmen, lightmen, soundmen, and, of course, reporters, all are necessary. To get this show on the road is a major effort requiring meticulous planning. The assignment editor wants to make sure the story is worth going after. It takes time to set up the cameras and other equipment and more time to dismantle them. A newspaper reporter can dash easily from one end of the city to the other, while a TV crew is hampered by its gear.

In the field, the news story is directed by the reporter or correspondent, who tells the cameramen what shots to take and whom he plans to interview. After the story is filmed, a messenger rushes the film back to the laboratory to be developed. The reporter then phones the assignment editor to tell him how the story came out and to find out if there is another assignment for him.

While the camera crews are in the field, the assignment editor, producers, and writers are conferring on what will be included in the evening news show. If three crews have been out on assignment, the producer, who can be compared to a newspaper managing editor, decides which of the stories are most important in terms of news value and visual interest. The winnowed-out items are then assigned to writers who take the information from the reporters in the field by phone. The purpose is to enable the writer to understand and edit the film. An associate producer tells the writer how long the film should be.

The newspaper writer has the satisfaction of having a column or more to tell an important story, but the TV newswriter has no such luxury. Truly significant events are frequently boiled down to thirty seconds of air-time. The problem of compressing five or six local stories into a fifteen-minute or even thirty-minute news show sometimes results in a choppy overview of the

Surrounded by mementos of major stories he has covered over the years, Walter Cronkite writes his daily report for CBS News.

news. There is seldom time for background information, and interviews, reports, etc., may be shown out of context in a way that sometimes makes it hard for the viewer to completely understand the story. It is in their news specials and documentaries that the TV networks and stations do their best job, particularly when dramatic film is available to underscore the narrative.

News by Radio

Although television news is still finding its way, its older brother, radio, has been around for considerably more years (the first national election returns were broadcast in Pittsburgh in 1920). Radio news became common in the 1930s and by World War II was a major source of public information. The late Edward R. Murrow became known throughout the world for his broadcasts from London during the German blitz. Several other war correspondents transmitted their reports by radio.

The predictions of radio's death with the advent of television in the late 1940s were highly premature. Instead of fading away as expected, the little box began broadcasting more news than ever. Radio is still the No. 1 medium for reaching people in their cars, at the beach, or while they're working at home, shops, or offices. Some stations, such as WINS and WCBS in New York, broadcast nothing but news and commercials. Scores of other stations program regular half-hour newscasts of one-, two-, or five-minute duration. In five minutes of uninterrupted time, an announcer can read off as many as twelve stories and, in some instances, do a better job on them than could television. These frequent news broadcasts do have one drawback. News normally does not change that rapidly, but radio stations feel compelled to freshen up each half-hour or hour presentation so it won't sound the same as the previous one. This involves a certain amount of artificial juggling of the order of the items as well as a cosmetic rewrite of them. Thus, the lead story at the 3:00 P.M. newscast—let's say it's about the dollar devaluation—is replaced at 4:00 P.M. by the resignation of a cabinet official, which was the third story read at 3:00 P.M. In other words, no new stories of importance developed between 3:00 and 4:00, but the station was concerned that listeners might lose interest and switch to another frequency if they heard the news repeated in the same style. Both radio and television will interrupt running programs with bulletins on major events such as a declaration of war, a political assassination, an historic court decision, or a great disaster.

Radio newswriters get the bulk of their material from the wires of the Associated Press or United Press International. The larger stations field reporters, but hundreds of others maintain a "rip 'n' read" news operation. The news is ripped off the AP or UPI teletype machines and read over the air, often with little or no editing. Both press associations have broadcast divisions which prepare news in conversational radio style. As they are for newspapers, press releases are another news source for radio. Elaboration of the news handouts and other local news can often be obtained over the telephone by more enterprising airways reporters.

As we shall see in another chapter, a number of newspapers also own radio and television stations. This arrangement has both good and bad aspects. On the minus side is the fact that it can lead to a news monopoly in cities with no other newspapers or broadcast stations. Not only is the news in the hands of one owner but editorial opinion, as well, is restricted to one voice. On the other hand, a sparsely staffed radio or TV station can benefit from the news coverage by the parent newspaper, as is true in several communities.

Magazine Journalism

Scores of magazine writers and editors are considered journalists. They work for such magazines as *Time, Newsweek, U.S. News & World Report, Harper's, Atlantic Monthly, The Nation, New Republic, The New York Times Magazine, Sports Illustrated, New York, National Review,* and *Reader's Digest.* These periodicals contain articles on subjects that have made newspaper headlines. The difference is in treatment. Whereas the newspaper plays the stories for their immediate news value, magazines take the same topic and give it depth and perspective. After the newsmaking confrontation between dissident Indians and government agents at Wounded Knee, South Dakota, *The New York Times Magazine* featured a long article explaining what the Indian bitterness was all about. Both *Harper's* and *Atlantic Monthly* carried pieces on President Richard Nixon's feud with the press, and *New York* Magazine has run several probing stories on such front-page fare as police corruption, the dollar pinch, the permissive society, and street mugging.

Time and *Newsweek* review the week's news, giving it a dash and color for which newspapers don't have time. For someone unable to read a newspaper every day, these two news magazines are ideal. Both have had a profound effect on American journalism by influencing newspaper writing style. The news feature story owes much of its popularity to its creation in *Time,* which began publishing in 1923.

From time to time, magazines make newspaper headlines by publishing exclusive articles of a startling nature. *Time* first exposed the John Birch Society. *Sports Illustrated* turned the spotlight on racketeers in boxing. Rachel Carson's *Silent Spring,* the best-selling book that revealed the environmental crisis, first appeared as a series of articles in *The New Yorker. Reader's Digest* produced a newsmaking report of a strong link between smoking and cancer.

REDBOOK

Beverly Waison (left), Assistant Beauty Editor of *Redbook,*
and Beauty Editor Jean Adams go over plans for an upcoming
beauty feature in the magazine's beauty salon.

These stories were in the muckraking tradition of magazine journalism in America. At the turn of the century, fearless periodicals such as *McClure's, Collier's, Arena,* and *Cosmopolitan* brought public attention to such scandals as unsanitary meat-packing firms, business piracy, worthless patent medicines, slum conditions, and political corruption. Today, this kind of journalism is called investigative reporting and its practitioners are avidly read in both magazines and newspapers.

The magazine writer has one distinct advantage over his newspaper counterpart. He has more time to search out facts, interview sources, and weigh his findings. He also has more space in which to relate his story, as much as seven or eight pages totaling four thousand to ten thousand words. On occasion, a magazine will devote an entire issue to one article, as *The New Yorker* did with the Hiroshima atom-bombing and *The New York Times Magazine* with Watergate. Many magazine writers who deal in topical journalism are current or former newspapermen and women such as J. Anthony Lukas, Gay Talese, Judith Crist, Lewis Lapham, Nora Ephron, Fred Powledge, Caroline Bird, Edwin Diamond, Dick Schaap, Fred Cook, and Terry Morris.

The magazines mentioned so far mostly fall in the general interest category. This is ironic in one sense. The present trend in the United States is away from the general consumer periodical to the special interest one. In recent years we have seen the death of *Life, Saturday Evening Post, Look, Collier's,* and several others which were less well known. *Look* folded with a circulation of 6,500,000, but with a $5 million revenue loss in one year. A drop in advertising receipts was instrumental in the disappearance of all the abovementioned magazines. Television siphoned off some of the advertising dollars as sponsors came to realize that the tube could provide them with an audience of twenty to sixty million, a figure that even the highest-circulation magazines like *Life* and *Look* could in no way ap-

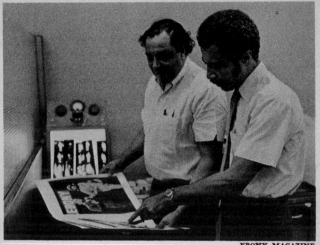

EBONY MAGAZINE

Herbert Nipson, Executive Editor of *Ebony* Magazine (right), and Managing Editor Hans J. Massaquoi discuss cover make-ups.

proach. However, the changing American society was an equally important factor. As income soared and leisure time increased in the post-World War II era, affluent Americans began to pursue special interests. Magazines slanted toward sports, recreation, travel, hobbies, automobiles, health, music, the performing arts, world affairs, and so on, started to flood the newsstands. Many perished shortly after birth but the trend continued and is still strong. Advertisers look fondly on these publications because they reach a specific kind of reader, a feat that is all but impossible to achieve on television with its mass audience. The manufacturer of power boats knows that his product is more likely to claim the attention of potential buyers in *Boating* than in a general interest magazine or on television. Ninety-seven new magazines emerged in the first eight months of 1973, virtually all of them aimed at a special readership. Recent arrivals have included a bevy of black-oriented magazines: *Jet, Essence,*

Black Enterprise, Black Sports, New Woman, Black World, and *Freedomways. Ebony,* the forerunner of most of these, seems now to be firmly established in the marketplace.

Tastes in magazines may fluctuate still more but there is no evidence that they are going out of style. Millions of copies are sold every day to people who seemingly cannot find a satisfactory replacement for their content on the TV screen. It appears equally certain that magazines will continue to play an important role in American journalism.

CHAPTER THREE

Media Ownership and Practice

THE UNITED STATES is one of the few countries in the world where no license is required to start a newspaper. Anyone with a printing machine can go into business tomorrow under the full protection of the Constitution, which forbids interference with a free press.

This is the theory. The realities are something else again. Publishing a newspaper today, even a small one, is enormously expensive. Launching a new daily in a metropolitan area requires a capital investment of at least $15 million, according to expert opinion. Few have undertaken such a venture in recent years. The trend, in fact, has been in the opposite direction. In the past twenty years, a number of daily newspapers have folded or merged with other papers in the same community. The losses have taken place in New York, Detroit, San Francisco, Los Angeles, Boston, Washington, D.C., Cleveland, Newark, Chicago, Oakland, and elsewhere. As late as 1962, New York had seven daily newspapers; today it has three. San Francisco went from four to two dailies in ten years. Only thirty-six American cities currently have two or more competing dailies. This means that hundreds of cities across the land are served by only one newspaper. These include some fairly large centers like Newark, Oakland, Buffalo, and Saginaw, Michigan. Many big cities have separate morning and evening papers under a single ownership, including Atlanta, Tucson, Indianapolis, Louisville, Tulsa, Kansas City, Richmond, Raleigh, Minneapolis, and Portland, Oregon. Most of these papers have separate editorial staffs and some take different political viewpoints.

The shrinkage in the number of newspapers stems from a combination of economic, social, and political conditions. One reason offered most frequently by the newspaper industry is the mounting cost of production. The owners also have charged that the craft unions have resisted automation processes which can cut production costs. This battle is still going on as newspapers seek to install computerized typesetting gadgets and other technological devices that save money but reduce manpower. Compromises on the issue have been reached between some newspapers and the unions, which have come to realize that the technology revolution is inevitable and may be a means of insuring the survival of the remaining newspapers. Automation already has taken over wholly or partially in a number of daily papers throughout the country.

The fading-away of the American newspaper from 2,042 dailies in 1920 to approximately 1,761 today was more than a simple matter of economics, however. An equally strong factor was the tremendous migration of people to the suburbs in the postwar period. The population shift led to the birth and growth of suburban dailies and weeklies which competed for readership with the metropolitan papers—very successfully in some areas. *Newsday* on Long Island with a circulation of half a million is a prime example of a suburban daily that thrived while New York City papers were going under. Major newspapers also suffered from the preference of advertisers for fewer competing newspapers and from the expansion of radio and television.

The period from 1920 to the present also saw the absorption of scores of individually and family-owned newspapers by chains or groups. A study by University of Minnesota Professor Raymond B. Nixon in 1971 revealed that half the nation's dailies—879—were owned by 157 newspaper groups. The Gannett Newspapers owned the most dailies, 44,* followed by the Thompson Newspapers with 43. They were trailed by the Scripps League Newspapers with 31, Donrey Media, 25, and Newhouse Newspapers, 22.

In total circulation, however, these chains lagged well behind the Chicago Tribune Company, which owns only eight newspapers. The explanation is that the Tribune Company's holdings include the *New York Daily News* with a circulation of over three million, the largest in the United States. The firm also publishes the *Chicago Tribune,* whose combined daily and Sunday circulation runs close to two million. Other large groups in terms of circulation and/or newspapers owned are Knight, Freedom, Ridder, Hearst, Times Mirror, Cowles, Dow Jones, Copley, Cox, Lee, Ingersoll, Harte-Hanks, Stauffer, and Speidel.

There is hardly a state in the Union which does not have one or more group-owned newspapers. There may be one in your hometown. Among cities with such dailies are Detroit, Miami, San Francisco, New York, St. Louis, Rochester (N.Y.), Denver, Syracuse, Newark, Ottumwa (Ia.), Mount Vernon (N.Y.), Muskegon (Mich.), and Boise (Id.). In most instances, the group's headquarters are far away in other cities. The Gannett corporation, for example, runs its huge chain from Rochester, New York, where it publishes its biggest daily, the *Rochester Times-Union.* Decisions affecting the entire group are often made at headquarters and passed down the line.

In the practice of some chains, the corporate orders include editorial policy as well as business procedures. The editorials of John S. Knight and W. R. Hearst frequently appear in the respective newspapers controlled by them. In contrast, Samuel Newhouse, another powerful chain magnate, allows his newspapers a great deal of editorial freedom as long as they continue to

---

* Gannett has since acquired nine more newspapers.

show a profit. The Newhouse attitude implies that the editors and managers on the scene know their community best and should be permitted to call the turns. It also assumes that the editors are professional newsmen who know what they're doing. This is important in the case of Newhouse and some other group chieftains who are primarily businessmen and not journalists. Still, the existence of even the most liberal of chains cannot dispel the fact that their newspapers have lost the individuality they had maintained as privately owned enterprises. Missing is the flavor once given them by an independent publisher or editor, however biased he might have been. In the days of personal journalism, readers always knew where editor-publishers such as Joseph Pulitzer, the elder William Randolph Hearst, James Gordon Bennett, and Robert R. McCormick stood.*

Group ownership does have one advantage for the readers of community dailies. The larger chains such as Knight, Newhouse, and Gannett are able to maintain bureaus in Washington and to send correspondents abroad. Thus, the subscriber benefits from a coverage that most small, independent dailies cannot afford. They do, of course, buy AP and UPI service, but this isn't the same as having one's own reporter on the scene. If, for example, a tiny daily in an agricultural community wants a special report on farm prices, the chain's man in Washington can track it down. Also, since the group's purchasing power is greater than that of an independent publisher, it can furnish its papers with syndicated features not ordinarily available to them. And the business side of these member-papers appreciates the fact that the group sales force is better able to attract national advertising to their pages.

It would be wrong to assume that because of the drop in the number of dailies in the past two decades the industry is in bad shape. Actually, it is among the

---

* These men owned, in order, the *St. Louis Post-Dispatch* and *New York World;* the Hearst Newspapers; the *New York Herald;* and the *Chicago Tribune.*

healthiest businesses in the country and it appears to
be getting even healthier. In 1973, the Audit Bureau of
Circulation, an independent agency, reported that combined daily and Sunday circulation in the United States
reached an average of 62,353,381 copies per issue in
1972, a gain of 610,240 over 1971 and the biggest
increase since 1960. Moreover, total newspaper advertising revenue in 1972 was about $7 billion com-
pared with slightly over $1 billion in 1946. The Ameri-
can Newspaper Publishers Association issued this
optimistic report in 1973:

Despite the problems of inflation and restraints imposed
by economic controls, daily newspapers in 1972 showed a
continuing strong posture in most areas which serve as in-
dicators of newspapers' economic strength. The prospect
of a healthy economy in 1973 promises a continuing growth
for daily newspapers. . . .

In 1972, daily newspapers continued their lead in advertising volume over other media, receiving 30.2 percent
of the advertising dollar. According to preliminary esti-
mates, total advertising for all media was $23.1 billion.
Newspapers' share was a record high of approximately
$7 billion.

Newspaper employment reached 380,500, an increase of
10,500 over 1971—a 53.1 percent increase since World
War II.

According to ANPA sources, investments for plant expansion and modernization by U.S. and Canadian daily
newspapers continued to show an increase in 1972. It is
estimated that this increase will be even greater in 1973. . . .

The newspapers' prosperity is not hard to fathom.
People still read and depend on them for information,
advertisers consider them a rewarding outlet, and they
are continually improving in content, makeup, and
sense of public responsibility. There will be more about
this in a later chapter.

If the stated facts have convinced you that advertising is vital to the existence of newspapers, you're

absolutely correct. Advertising revenue keeps newspapers in business. Without it, few dailies or weeklies
would long survive. Subscription and street sale earn-
ings account for only a fraction of what it takes to
keep a newspaper going. A newspaper's advertising
department is constantly engaged in selling space.

Because of the importance of the ad dollar, one
question is bound to arise. Do advertisers, especially
the big ones, influence the editorial content of newspapers? There is no flat answer. Anyone who takes the
time and trouble can surely discover instances of certain newspapers whose news accounts or editorials have
been tailored to the interests of advertisers. The
Columbia Journalism Review and other publications
that criticize the news media have cited some rather
flagrant examples. At one time Detroit newspapers
trod carefully where the automobile industry, the economic mainstay of that city, was concerned. A San
Francisco newspaper was perhaps overly kind in reporting the European tour of a department store magnate who had little to say about it that was interesting,
amusing, or informative. Some small-town dailies and
weeklies go out of their way to run "puff" stories about
merchants' "dollar days" and other commercial enterprises.

But to say that advertisers routinely determine news
content would be the grossest kind of overstatement.
In city rooms across the country, editors are assigning
stories and reporters are writing them without ever giving a thought to what an advertiser might think. There
are editors who would throw an advertising manager
out of their offices if he attempted to win favors for
his clients. A Pittsburgh department store owner who
withdrew his advertising from a local newspaper because he disagreed with its news policies had to go, hat
in hand, to the paper's editor to have it restored. Newspapers can afford this kind of independence because
advertisers need them as much as they need advertisers.
Department stores, supermarkets, and other establish-
ments continue to find the newspaper the best medium

for promoting their wares. A thirty-second TV commercial flashes on and then is gone, perhaps forever. A newspaper reader can refer again and again to an ad, a key element for stores listing multiple products and prices. There is also the fact that newspaper ad space is cheaper than television time.

The oil industry is a case in point of the ability of newspapers to resist advertising pressure and influence. Since the cleaning-up of the environment became big news, the oil companies have been targeted as one of the major polluters of air and water. Newspapers carry reams of oil-product advertising without being a bit hesitant about printing stories about oil pollution. Every time an oil leak washes over a beach or an oil company is cited for fouling the skies, the facts appear in newspapers across the land.

Other companies, too, have learned that their advertising dollars cannot spare them embarrassing publicity. Recently, a leading brokerage firm was charged by the government with illegal practices. All three New York City newspapers gave the story a big play, although they had frequently accepted advertising from the company. Cigarette manufacturers continue to buy advertising space despite the numerous stories that have appeared relating smoking to cancer. In fact, R. J. Reynolds Industries, a tobacco firm, led the list of the 10 top national advertisers in newspapers during 1972, spending $35,240,500. General Motors and Ford were second and third respectively in the rating compiled by Media Records, Inc. GM bought $32,622,600 worth of space and Ford $21,499,000. Yet this did not stop newspapers from printing stories—several of them on page one—when the automobiles of these companies were recalled for repair of defective parts. Other big national advertisers were Trans World Airlines ($8,-518,000) and American Airlines ($5,345,900). Their revenue, however, did not keep air accidents out of the press.

The advertising coin also has a reverse side. A number of newspapers and broadcast stations maintain standards of taste and ethics which advertisers must meet to have their ads or commercials accepted. Several newspapers, for example, turn away ads by fortune tellers, massage parlors, and producers of dubious products. TV stations will not run liquor commercials.

In recent years, a growing list of newspapers has rejected or modified advertisements for X-rated movies. A recent survey conducted by the Pennsylvania Newspaper Publishers Association revealed that 63 of 76 state newspapers accept X-rated film ads but delete words or artwork they consider offensive. Eleven papers said they flatly refuse any ads for X-rated pictures. Such policies constitute censorship and have been assailed by liberals. The media's usual reply is that they serve a cross section of the population and therefore must exercise caution to avoid offending any segment of their audience.

The Wire Services

Most Americans get news of what's happening outside their communities from the wires of the Associated Press or United Press International. These giant wire agencies have no newspapers or broadcast stations of their own. They sell their services to newspaper, television, radio, and other clients throughout the world. Hundreds of AP and UPI reporters and editors man bureaus around the globe and send their stories over leased wires. As pointed out earlier, only the big metropolitan dailies and the networks can afford to keep staff members in Washington and abroad and even they cannot match the coverage of the wire services. Smaller news media cannot compete in this field and rely on the press associations for foreign and a great deal of domestic reporting. (A 1973 survey commissioned by consumer activist Ralph Nader disclosed that of the 1,749 daily newspapers in the United States at that time, only 478, or 27 percent, had their own Washington correspondents. Of 799 television stations, only 31,

Walter Mears, AP Assistant Bureau Chief in Washington, D.C. (foreground), writes leads on the 1972 Presidential Election returns.

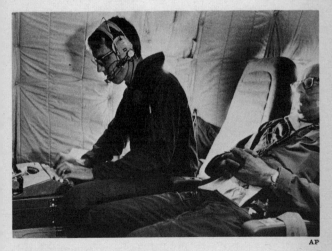

Aboard an Air Force research plane, Los Angeles AP science writer Bill Stockton writes about a total eclipse of the sun over the Arctic Circle, which he witnessed during the flight. Napping in the seat next to him is one of the Los Alamos, New Mexico, scientists.

or 4 percent, had their own Washington reporters, while only 46 of the 6,377 radio stations were represented in the capital by their own correspondents).

Wire service writing is characterized by a straight, unvarnished style. Since they serve so many different customers with widely varying political and social outlooks, both AP and UPI have put heavy stress on complete objectivity. Stories contain little in the way of interpretation, although the two agencies maintain separate staffs for feature and in-depth writing.

The Associated Press, whose roots go back to 1848, is primarily a membership organization administered by a general manager selected by a board of directors. The board is made up of eighteen member-publishers who serve three-year terms. AP's more than eight thousand members pay for the news service according to their size and circulation. *The New York Times* is charged more for the service than, say, the St. Joseph (Mo.) *News-Press*. AP members are obligated to share their local news with the wire service but the latter generates most of the reports it transmits on its wires and by radio. The Associated Press maintains 58 bureaus in the United States and 111 abroad. Its foreign outposts include a number of native reporters and part-time correspondents, in addition to American staffers sent there from the United States.

AP's chief competitor is United Press International, which was founded in 1907 as the United Press Associations. It trailed AP in size and scope until 1958, when it absorbed a smaller wire agency, International News Service, which had been owned by the Hearst Corporation. With this acquisition, UP became UPI and a strong rival of the older Associated Press. Both agencies are similar in structure and each spends about $70 million a year in collecting and transmitting news.

UPI is a private, profit-making corporation that sells its services to clients on a contract basis. Like AP, the payment rate is based on the news medium's size and audience. UPI has been noted for its lively writing style and the enterprise of its reporters. It also was the

UPI

A portion of the newsroom at the United Press International headquarters in New York. The editors who man the general news desk (upper right) read dispatches transmitted on national news circuits and circulate the stories to domestic papers.

first wire agency to furnish news for radio, which now relies heavily on both services. The Associated Press changed its rather stodgy writing style several years ago to meet UPI's challenge of a brisk, sometimes casual approach to momentous events. Both services have a number of outstanding reporters, who have won scores of journalistic awards.

Is one service better than the other? This can be decided only on a story or bureau basis. UPI, which opened its foreign service in Latin America, is considered somewhat stronger in that region. AP is perhaps a shade superior in reporting from Europe. But these are generalities. Individual newsmen and women from both agencies have scored exclusive beats in all corners of the world.

In addition to news in words, AP and UPI transmit pictures by an electronic process that takes only seconds. Also, both services are switching over rapidly to technological advances that will speed words and photos even faster. UPI announced that it was installing electronic editing processes in all of its one hundred U.S. news bureaus. With this system, reporters can type copy on a video-typewriter that requires no paper. The words appear on a screen and can be edited electronically as well.

The press associations put a premium on fast, accurate writing. The pace is more hectic than on a newspaper, where reporters may relax between editions. Wire service copy is constantly being updated as news breaks. An AP or UPI reporter or rewrite man may turn out five or more new leads on one major story such as the Watergate hearings, the return of Juan Peron to Argentina, or new fighting in Southeast Asia. A newspaper must wait for a new edition before it can run a revised story but the wire agencies can shoot the news out as fast as it happens.

News judgment is an important quality for a wire service writer. With thousands of words flowing into UPI and AP control centers from bureaus around the world, editors and rewrite men must screen the copy

AP

CRTs (cathode ray tubes), electronic editing and writing units, are shown in operation at the Associated Press General News Desk in New York.

carefully. The UPI cable desk in New York, for example, gets about 90,000 words a day from Europe and Africa, up to 50,000 from Asia, about 15,000 from South America, and, when the General Assembly is in session, about 30,000 words from the United Nations.

Stanley M. Swinton, vice-president and director of world services for the Associated Press, has written this description of the organization's current global operation:

News and newsphotos are being distributed internationally by the Associated Press to more nations, in more detail, more accurately and faster than ever before in history from a single source. Over one billion people a day make their value judgments on international developments on the basis of AP news.

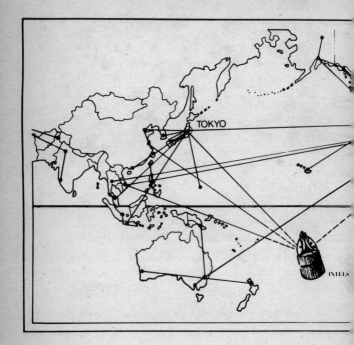

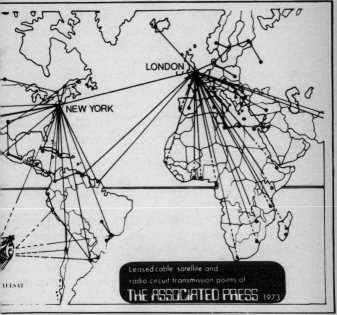

Leased cable, satellite and radio circuit transmission points of THE ASSOCIATED PRESS 1973

AP

Newspaper editors in Buenos Aires or Singapore can go to press with the same stories carried by European or New York editions of the same hour.

Radio and television stations in Latin America, the Middle East and Africa can transmit news bulletins simultaneously with broadcasters in the U.S.A., Asia and Europe.

In some nations with weak internal communication, interior newspapers and broadcasters are able to provide their readers and listeners with better coverage of international events than of developments in their own country.

Even newspaper and broadcasting professionals often do not fully appreciate the dramatic and far-reaching growth and changes in mass distribution of news and pictures overseas since the end of World War II.

The Associated Press, the oldest and largest international press association, provides news and photos to more than 10,000 newspapers and broadcast stations in over 104 countries. . . .

Physically, New York is the AP control center, but in practice AP is a truly international press association, with communications facilities stretching around the world, the representatives deployed wherever news is breaking.

Both London and Tokyo play key roles as regional control centers.

From New York, cable, radio-teletype and satellite circuits operate around the clock transmitting news east, west and south.

The news file to Asia is carried by landline to San Francisco, then by submarine cable to Tokyo. At Tokyo there is a powerful radio-teletype relay which boosts the signal into the Philippines, Korea, Vietnam, Thailand, Malaysia, Indonesia, Burma and other countries of Southeast Asia. Tokyo has editorial control of the Asian circuit from New York and directly relays Asian regional news.

The basic world news file simultaneously is transmitted to London by trans-Atlantic cable. In London a powerful relay boosts the signal and beams it to the mid-East, South Asia and Africa. Separate beams insure optimum reception in each area. London takes over editorial control from New York from time to time to directly relay regional material.

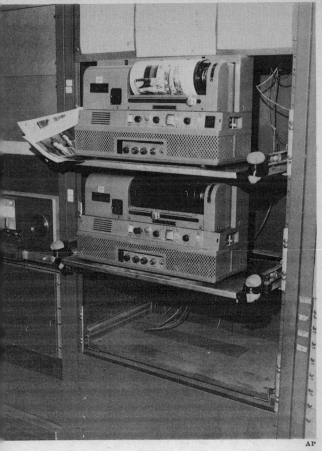

AP

An Associated Press wirephoto transmitter in New York

Meanwhile the news file for Europe and the British Isles is flowing into London from New York over a leased cable. There it is refiled into a teleprinter network controlled by editors in London and covering Europe just as the AP's domestic wires cover the United States. It goes to Paris, Geneva, Zurich, Frankfurt, Berlin, Bonn, Copenhagen, Oslo, Stockholm, Helsinki, Madrid, Milan, Rome, Naples, Vienna, Moscow, Budapest, Belgrade, Sofia, Brussels, Amsterdam, Prague, Bucharest and other major cities.

In Western Europe the news is received in each capital, translated into the language of the country and then put into separate national teleprinter networks. Italy is an example. An AP leased wire network within the country transmits the news in Italian to Naples, Rome, Florence, Bologna, Milan, Leghorn, Genoa, Turin, Bergamo, Brescia, Venice, Trieste, Bari, Messina, Catania, Palermo and other leading cities. . . .

In addition to news wires, the AP maintains a permanent, leased wire newsphoto network linking the major European capitals and major provincial centers. This was the first such network established in Europe and is constantly expanding. Today the network extends from London to nineteen European nations, going as far east as Moscow and as far south as Naples.

Pictures are transmitted to and from the United States and Europe over the first trans-Atlantic cablephoto circuit ever to have operated under twenty-four-hour-a-day permanent lease. The AP also operates the world's only photo computer, which permits a direct hook-up between the American newsphoto network and those in other countries which operate at a different speed.

Within Europe, AP bureaus schedule and put stories on the news wires as they do in the United States. Rome will advise London it has a four-hundred-word story ready. London will call in the story, and pipe it through the cable into New York. Thus, when the story is signed off by the operator in Rome, it has been delivered simultaneously to the European capitals and to New York, which quickly relays it to the world. Utilizing satellite circuits, the same procedure is used in Latin America.

With its vast network of radio-teletype, satellite and cable circuits, the AP can deliver a bulletin in less than one minute to over 104 countries. This speed, made possible by the constant adoption of new techniques and equipment, increases the necessity for responsible, careful reporting. It is harder today than ever before for a correction to catch up with the original story. That is why the AP puts the highest possible premium on accuracy.

Outside of Europe, AP bureaus receive the news by cable, satellite or radio-teletype and distribute it by local teleprinter circuits or by messenger. Thousands of papers and broadcasters—especially those in outlying areas of Africa, Asia and Latin America—do their own receiving on their own equipment. Countries with deficient local communications often learn of major domestic developments through the AP's international news report before hearing about them from their own capitals.

The system is basically the same in Latin America, where AP serves over six hundred subscribers. Spanish, rather than English, is used as the basic language for the report, and a special English-language transmission is used to service newspapers and broadcasters in the Caribbean.

Most of those who prepare the material for transmission have worked abroad for many years. All strive constantly to familiarize themselves with the news needs of editors throughout the world. For a man with experience in Africa or Europe it takes extensive study to know the needs and problems of other areas.

Logs reporting what stories are being used and at what length are radioed or cabled to New York each day from the major capitals.

An hour after Tokyo AP first editions hit the street, for example, the New York desk has a breakdown of every story on Tokyo front pages, the source, the subject, and the need for followups.

One of the criticisms of the wire service story is its almost standardized form, which makes for a sameness in newspapers throughout the nation. The wire services also supply newspapers with many features, including comic strips, puzzles, columns, etc. One can move from Tampa, Florida, to Spokane, Washington, and find the newspaper pretty much the same in terms of wire service content. Too few local newspapers attempt to develop homegrown features produced by their own staff members. Many young and middle-aged reporters are denied the chance to initiate features because their publishers prefer syndicated material that may not be as good. New "Reporter Power" in the news media may change such attitudes, as we shall learn later in the book.

Broadcast Ownership

Former Vice-President Spiro T. Agnew kicked up a storm of controversy when he said in a 1969 speech: "The American people should be made aware of the trend toward monopolization of the great public information vehicles and the concentration of more and more power over public opinion in fewer and fewer hands."

Critics quickly pointed out that Agnew was simply reflecting the hostility of the Nixon administration to the press. It was known that the administration objected to the "instant analyses" given by network commentators immediately following a presidential speech. Television and newspaper reporters also had noted that the tendency of President Nixon was to withdraw from the press even though he had promised an "open administration."

Agnew's remarks, however, did focus attention on the concentration of media ownership in the United States. Even liberals, who had no love for Agnew or Richard Nixon, thought that the former Vice-President might have a point, albeit for the wrong reasons. Stephen R. Barnett, a University of California law professor who specializes in media, wrote later in the *Nation:*

Concentration of ownership is a dominant fact of press and broadcasting operation in this country. Newspaper chains now control more than half the nation's daily newspapers (and more than 60 percent of the circulation) and are fast acquiring the rest. And there are some 93 instances in some 85 cities where the owner of a daily newspaper also owns the local TV station.

To carry the idea a step further, almost all nation-wide network programming is produced by three major corporations serving hundreds of affiliate stations throughout the country. Whether the networks completely determine TV and radio content is another matter, which will be examined in a moment. But it is true that most of what we see on television originates with the following networks: the National Broadcasting Company, the Columbia Broadcasting System, and the American Broadcasting Company. From their studios in New York or Los Angeles are broadcast the quiz programs, the situation comedies, the made-for-TV movies, the talk shows, the soap operas, and the news. Network-affiliated stations, most of which are separately owned, create little of their own programming, although the larger independents do offer local newscasts usually directly before or after the network feed of world and national news by such stars as Walter Cronkite, John Chancellor, Roger Mudd, Howard K. Smith, and Harry Reasoner.

As cited earlier, news constitutes a relatively small segment of network programming, most of which is taken up with entertainment. In fact, television and radio are just two of the enterprises owned by the networks, which are gigantic public corporations.

The Columbia Broadcasting Co., Inc., is a huge conglomerate whose various enterprises range from broadcasting to toy manufacturing. The corporation operates the CBS network and owns and operates five TV stations. Its holdings also include the publishing firm of Holt, Rinehart and Winston, Inc.; CBS Records; CBS Musical Instruments; six business and technical schools; a construction firm; research laboratories; a publications division that publishes magazines, including *Field and Stream;* and two paperback book houses. In 1972, the CBS Television Network was the largest advertising medium in the nation for the nineteenth consecutive year. Total net sales for the corporation were $1,403,-184,000.

CBS's chief rival, the National Broadcasting Co., is in the same league. NBC, however, is a division of a still larger organization, Radio Corporation of America, whose 1972 sales reached $3.86 billion. RCA is involved in space and defense business, electronics, vehicle renting (Hertz), publishing (Random House), real estate, global communications, records, home products, and other commercial products and services. Revenues from NBC and RCA Global Communications totaled $820 million in 1972, a year in which NBC counted 600 television advertisers.

The smallest of the "Big Three" is small only by comparison. The American Broadcasting Co. recorded revenues of $869,449,000 in 1972, the most successful year in the company's history. ABC is not as diversified as its two chief competitors but it does own and operate five television stations, four radio networks, seven radio stations, a chain of theaters, a record division, three farm publications, and two scenic and wildlife centers in Florida.

Metromedia, the fourth largest television company, has six TV stations and twelve radio stations in metropolitan markets. It also comprises Metromedia Producers Corporation, Holiday on Ice, Metro Records, and many other divisions.

Next in line is Group W (for Westinghouse), which includes twelve TV and radio stations. The parent firm, Westinghouse Electric Corporation, is one of the nation's largest appliance and electronics manufacturers. The company also builds power systems, housing developments, and nuclear reactors.

Each of the three main networks has about two hundred affiliated stations, including eight to ten which they own and operate. The affiliates around the country sign contracts with the networks giving them the right to the network feed. "Prime time" programming, from 7:00 to 10:00 P.M., is usually supplied by the networks from Maine to Alaska. The affiliates, however, are not obligated to show any particular network show, and occasions arise when a station in Kansas City or Grand Rapids (Mich.) has refused to pass on a network program that it considers too controversial or offensive to the moral standards of the community.

In March, 1973, CBS postponed its scheduled telecast of *Sticks and Bones,* an antiwar play about a blinded Vietnam veteran. The network acted after it had encountered massive objections from many of its affiliates and even from two of its owned-and-operated stations. The drama was to have been shown at the time the Vietnam prisoners of war were returning to the United States, a motivating factor in the adverse reaction. Robert D. Wood, president of the CBS television network, said of the dispute: "The play's presentation on the air at this time might be unnecessarily abrasive to the feelings of millions of Americans whose lives or attention are at the moment emotionally dominated by the returning POWs and other veterans who have suffered the ravages of war."

CBS's decision was branded as "corporate cowardice" by the American Civil Liberties Union, which added that the postponement "interferes with both the right of the creative artists involved and the public's right to view a dramatic production dealing with an important social issue."

The play was presented over the CBS network the following August, with some affiliate stations still declining to show it. In an earlier case, eleven CBS affiliates refused to carry a movie telecast of the Broadway hit, *Who's Afraid of Virginia Woolf?,* because of its sexual allusions and "inappropriate language." Sixteen other affiliated stations delayed the presentation in order to take it out of prime time. Affiliates of all three major networks have banned various programs for one reason or another. This reflects a mid-America conservatism that network officials take into consideration in all program planning. Of all the media, the broadcast industry is most sensitive to public opinion.

A paramount reason for this sensitivity is the Federal Communications Commission (FCC), the government agency which regulates broadcasting. When the Founding Fathers drew up the Constitution there was no radio or television, nor were these instruments foreseen. So, only freedom of the *press* is spelled out in the First Amendment, although broadcasters and others believe that the Constitution should be interpreted to cover freedom of the airwaves as well. The FCC is forbidden by law to act as a censoring organization but, in a sense, it exercises such power because it can and does determine who does and does not get a license to broadcast.

Congress established the FCC in 1934 on the theory that the airwaves belong to the people. But there is also a very practical reason for government control of channels and frequencies. Their availability is limited and if they were not allocated by the FCC there would be a disorderly scramble for them by private investors. With no regulation, perhaps four or five stations would compete for one TV channel, creating chaos on the air.

The FCC consists of a seven-man board appointed by the President for seven-year terms. The agency is empowered to regulate broadcast licenses, frequency assignments, power, operation time, and other technical aspects. It does not control advertising rates, profits, or internal management of the stations. Networks are not licensed but they obviously have a keen interest in licensing since there would be no networks without stations to carry their programs.

Television and radio licenses, according to FCC regulations, must be awarded on the basis of which applicant will best serve the public interest. Broadcasting is a big and profitable business. There have been as many as twelve contenders for one vacant TV channel. Licenses must be renewed periodically, but the FCC rarely revokes one. Public interest programming is a broad term that includes news reports, public safety announcements, armed forces commercials, and community activity reports. Some small-town radio stations play records all day long, except for a few news and weather reports, and manage to meet FCC standards. Similarly, television is not noted for its devotion to public interest fare. A few years ago, Newton N. Minow, former FCC chairman, labeled TV a "vast wasteland" and urged that the Commission use its influence to encourage better programs.

This issue is still being debated. The Communications Act of 1934 forbids the FCC to censor or obstruct the broadcasting of any individual program on the ground that its content is objectionable. It also prevents the Commission from assigning broadcast licenses "on the basis of the social, political or economic views embodied in their programs, or on any other arbitrary basis." However, the act does permit the FCC to make "reasonable judgments" as to the nature of the broadcasting service in terms of public interest and hand out licenses on such assessment.

There are signs that the FCC is getting tougher. In 1972, the Commission lifted the license of WHDH-TV, a Boston station owned by the *Herald-Traveler*, a newspaper in that city. The paper went out of business shortly after losing the station which, it maintained, had supported it financially. The FCC said it had acted in the interests of reducing concentration of media control in one city. The explanation did not satisfy many critics, who claimed the Commission ruling further reduced the number of newspapers in Boston to two. Unfazed, the FCC has proposed stringent new regulations to prevent the monopolization of the communications media. The Commission would:

1. Block any new combination of radio and television control of the same urban marketing area.

2. Take another look at a 1968 Justice Department

recommendation that many multimedia combinations now in existence be broken up.

3. Require current broadcast licensees to reduce their holdings, within five years, to a single mass medium in a single community. A private party could own an AM-FM radio combination, a TV station, or a newspaper—*but only one of the three.*

The FCC plan, which at this writing is still in the discussion stage, has provoked a swirl of controversy. Combination media owners are fighting it tooth and nail, along with the American Newspaper Publishers Association (ANPA) and the National Association of Broadcasters (NAB), the trade organizations which represent the interests of media owners. The NAB alone has spent $300,000 battling the proposal, which would break up about 90 newspaper-TV combinations and some 230 newspaper-radio linkups around the country.

In theory, the FCC proposition is a good one that could benefit the public by providing more voices in the community. In practice, the worth of the idea would depend on who would get the broadcast stations and newspapers that their present owners would have to release. If the new holders are responsible, public-spirited individuals, it could mean a bright future for mass communications in the United States. If, on the other hand, the beneficiaries of the FCC ruling are profit-hungry businessmen who couldn't care less about their public obligations, the regulation would be a waste of time. Clearly, new broadcasting licensees must be chosen with extreme caution. There is nothing wrong with making money in the media unless the proprietors short-change the public of what it is entitled to in a free society. Newspapers, television, and radio serve the people best when they offer an outlet for differing opinions, give minority groups and other less affluent citizens access to the media, and provide a variety of public service programming that both informs the audience and helps improve the quality of life.

Actually, opposing voices are now allowed access to the broadcasting media under the FCC's so-called "Fairness Doctrine." TV and radio stations featuring spokesmen for one side of a controversial issue must allow dissident viewpoints to be heard. The doctrine, which itself has been the target of criticism from the broadcast industry, was settled in favor of the FCC by the United States Supreme Court in the "Red Lion" case in 1969.

The landmark decision involved the Red Lion Broadcasting Company, the licensee of radio station WGCB in Red Lion, Pennsylvania. On November 27, 1964, the station presented a program called "Christian Crusade," part of a syndicated series by Billy James Hargis, a conservative evangelist. Hargis attacked Fred J. Cook, the author of the book, *Goldwater—Extremist on the Right,* an unflattering portrait of U.S. Senator Barry Goldwater, of Arizona. Hargis charged that Cook had been fired by a New York newspaper for making false accusations against city officials, that he had worked for a communist-sponsored magazine, and that he had smeared the late FBI director, J. Edgar Hoover.

Cook demanded the right to reply under the "Fairness Doctrine" and was refused by the station. The author appealed to the FCC, which ordered Red Lion to give him air-time. Again the station said "No" and Cook took the matter to the U.S. Court of Appeals, which ruled in his favor. The Supreme Court sustained the decision in 1969. Here is part of the opinion written by Justice Byron R. White:

It is the right of the viewers and listeners, not the right of the broadcasters, which is paramount. . . . It is the purpose of the First Amendment to preserve an uninhibited market place of ideas in which truth will ultimately prevail, rather than to countenance monopolization of that market, whether it be by the government itself or a private licensee. . . .

It is the right of the public to receive suitable access to social, political, esthetic, moral and other ideas and experiences which is crucial here. That right may not constitutionally be abridged either by Congress or by the FCC.

CBS, NBC, and the Radio and Television News Directors Association (RTNDA) all opposed the FCC position in briefs submitted to the courts. *Broadcasting* Magazine commented that the industry's opposition to the ruling was "the culmination of an all-out effort to knock out the rules and, if possible, undermine the doctrine itself."

What bothers the broadcasters about the "Fairness Doctrine" is that newspapers are under no such compulsion to provide space to opposing voices. A newspaper can print ten editorials or columns in a row condemning a politician or Congressional bill without having to give objectors a chance to reply. In actuality, many newspapers *do* provide forums for different views, but *they don't have to,* under the First Amendment privilege. The broadcasters want the same kind of Constitutional protection. Their position was summed up in this statement by NBC News Correspondent Bill Monroe before a U.S. Senate Subcommittee on Constitutional Rights on February 16, 1972:

We have a double standard for the First Amendment. The broadcaster must apply to a government body every three years for the right to stay in business. The publisher does not. If a news program stirs up a public or official criticism, the broadcaster may get a letter from a government commission directing him to explain and justify the program within twenty days. The publisher does not answer to any governmental body. The broadcaster is prevented, by statutory conditions, from presenting a debate among major candidates for the political enlightenment of his audience. The publisher is not. The cumulative restraints and inhibitions create an uneasy atmosphere which is hard for anybody outside of broadcasting to appreciate. . . .

In the Red Lion case, the high court said that government fairness "enhances rather than abridges the freedoms of speech and press protected by the First Amendment." The court's "enhancement" took away from the broadcaster a right held basic by every newspaper editor: his right to decide issues of fairness without government guidelines or government referees. . . .

On October 11, 1972, Julian Goodman, NBC president, declared in a speech at the University of Southern California:

Each advocate and partisan sees television through the personal filter of his own convictions and aspirations, and regards that distorted picture as the true image of what television is presenting. Since controversy—political and other—necessarily involves strongly divided views, television's treatment of controversy on any given question is likely to be considered biased by half of those concerned. The only comfort we can take is that the subjects and the sides keep changing, and over the long run, we come out about even. But in this environment, a system in which the government undertakes to assure "fairness" in reporting on controversy cannot help the performance of broadcasting's difficult and sensitive task. It can only undermine it. . . .

In 1973, NBC appealed an FCC staff ruling that its news special, "Pensions: The Broken Promise," violated the fairness doctrine. The Commission asserted that the program was not sufficiently "balanced." At about the same time, the American Medical Association asked the FCC to investigate alleged "distortion" in an NBC television documentary called "What Price Health?" The AMA demanded equal time to respond to what it termed a "personal attack" on that organization.

The broadcasting industry is not alone in its conviction that it should be free of government interference in its programming. Support has come from newspapers, scholars, and other groups. The Roscoe

Pound-American Trial Lawyers Foundation adopted a resolution that TV and radio stations be freed of all government control of their broadcasting, including requirements for political balance and fairness on issues.

Broadcasters also see a threat from another quarter —the White House. Clay T. Whitehead, director of the White House Office for Telecommunications Policy, has drafted legislation that would allow stations certain long-wanted concessions, while at the same time clamping down harder on programming. If adopted, the bill would eliminate some of the technical obstacles to obtaining license renewal and extend the FCC license term from three to five years. These provisions are pleasing to broadcasters; it's the second part of the bill that worries them.

Whitehead warned that the plan would also make local stations totally responsible for the news, commercial, and entertainment content of programs furnished them by the networks. He made his point clear when he complained of lack of "balance and objectivity" in network news programming and accused some reporters of "ideological plugola." In effect, he was telling local stations they could censor network programs and documentaries if they find them lacking in objectivity. Whitehead's views reflected a long-standing administration complaint that network news shows are dominated by eastern "elitist" liberals who do not speak for most Americans. This charge will be enlarged upon in another chapter on problems common to both the print and broadcast media.

Network news faces a challenge from another source: cable TV. Still in its infancy, cable television could account for 100 new channels to drastically alter TV news structure in the United States. Cable now reaches 7,000,000 homes and may fan out to 15,000,000 in the next few years. Teleprompter Corporation, the nation's largest cable company, is, at this writing, making plans for network programming to independent stations over the United States. The cable

TV industry has received a White House blessing and a promise from President Nixon that the government will help it achieve its full potential in the communications field. In a message to the twenty-second annual convention of the National Cable Television Association in 1973, the President warmed the hearts of delegates by saying that cable TV "with its abundant channel capacity can greatly expand the diversity of programming. With the opening of additional cable channels to local groups, programs can be more responsive to the needs of the community."

The next few years should be interesting ones in the broadcasting industry for broadcasters and viewers alike.

CHAPTER FOUR

Freedom Plus Responsibility

The liberty of the press is indeed essential to the nature of a free state; but this consists in laying no previous restraints upon publications, and not in freedom from censure for criminal matters when published. Every free man has an undoubted right to lay what sentiments he pleases before the public; to forbid this is to destroy the freedom of the press; but if he publishes what is improper, mischievous or illegal, he must take the consequences of his own temerity.

—Blackstone's Commentaries

Whatever else one may say about the newspaper business, self-examination is one of its virtues. Searching questions about right conduct or wrong conduct are put whenever journalists gather.

—Marquis W. Childs,
newspaper columnist

The first duty of a newspaper is to be accurate. If it be accurate, it follows that it is fair.

—Herbert Bayard Swope,
newspaper editor

IF THERE IS one institution (besides government) that Americans feel free to criticize, it is the press. Whether it be New York City or Sandusky, Ohio, citizens are

quick to analyze, condemn, or praise the media in private conversations, in public forums, or in letters to the
editor. Sometimes, displeasure with a newspaper, magazine, or broadcast station will take the form of a civil
libel suit in the courts. In earlier days, some editors
were caned, horsewhipped, and even murdered by outraged citizens. The Reverend Elijah Parish Lovejoy,
publisher of an Abolitionist weekly in Alton, Illinois,
was shot to death in 1837 by an angry mob which
previously had wrecked his printing press. A few weekly editors today have been harassed and their newspaper plants damaged by opponents of their editorial
views.

A nonviolent evaluation of press performance is, of
course, part of the democratic system. People have
every right to complain about a newspaper or broadcasting station which supplies them with most of their
information about current events. In addition, modern
theories hold that the press must be responsible as well
as free; that it has an obligation to be objective, fair,
and accurate. The media may be business but they're
not the same as a soap factory. Except for stockhold-
ers, the public is generally barred from intervening in
the management or internal policies of a soap factory.
It's different with a news organization. People are entitled to demand better conduct and performance if that
organization consistently disseminates false or distorted
information.

At the same time, it should be understood that newspapers and other media are run by professionals who
are trained to make judgments under deadline pressure.
What may seem to the layman as a case of bias or
distortion is not necessarily so regarded by editors or
reporters. They know, for example, that persons representing one side of a controversy were perhaps unavailable or declined to comment. Also, many readers
perceive the news with their own prejudices and therefore find nothing fair that does not agree with their
own views.

This seems to be a good place to list and then discuss the principal objections against the media. They are as follows:

1. Slanting or bias in news stories
2. Inaccuracy
3. One-sided editorial policy
4. Sensationalism
5. Overplaying crime news
6. Not enough local news
7. Not enough national and foreign news
8. Too much bad news

Is the News Slanted?

A 1972 study at the University of Wisconsin Mass Communications Research Center found that Wisconsin readers considered their newspapers to be biased and generally opposed to their opinions. The research was in connection with the news stories about student demonstrations at the university's Madison campus. According to the study, readers generally sided with the university and government authorities against the students and thought, sometimes inaccurately, that the newspapers slanted stories and headlines in favor of the demonstrators.

The Wisconsin conclusions support other studies on the same subject. There are millions of Americans who believe, rightly or wrongly, that the media are not giving them a true and honest picture. One reason, as indicated a moment ago, is that a number of readers and viewers react to news in terms of their own deeply held convictions. An individual with strong fundamentalist religious beliefs is apt to regard a story on sex education in schools as biased. A freethinker may see the media as a tool of the religious establishment.

This, however, does not disguise the fact that news slanting does exist. In some cases the slanting is by design. In others, it is inadvertent. To the reader, it probably doesn't make any difference. He is happy or unhappy on the basis of what he sees in print.

Slanting or bias by intent is not common and is becoming more rare. The sin is committed by publishers and editors who have an ax to grind on some issue. The bias is usually revealed in the news play rather than in the way stories are written. A San Francisco newspaper, for example, felt there was waste and inefficiency in the operation of a new rapid transit system. News supporting this belief was usually given front-page display, while the positive accomplishments of the transit line were given less prominence. The newspaper thought it was acting in the public interest in pointing out mismanagement, and it was. Those favoring the transportation company got another impression, however.

Three of the biggest stories in recent times have all drawn criticism of the news media for alleged bias and distortion. When Senator Thomas Eagleton was forced to resign as Democratic vice-presidential candidate in the 1972 election because of past treatment for mental illness, the press gave the story tremendous play. Newspapers ran banner headlines on the affair and some TV news shows devoted almost half their total time-slot to Eagleton. Many Democrats blamed the media for Eagleton's resignation, charging that the story was built up out of all proportion to its news value. A distinguished political scientist said after one TV news program dominated by the Eagleton matter: "If I were McGovern [George McGovern, the Democratic presidential candidate], I'd be furious." Edwin Diamond, a contributing editor to *New York* Magazine and a media specialist, observed about the Eagleton coverage: "Certainly there was a real story, somewhere under all the layers of media events. But the key questions—is mental depression like the flu, or are people susceptible again like heart attack victims? Was Senator Eagleton's real illness his ambition?—were never properly answered. Instead, the public was treated to nose counting (is he hurting the ticket?) and scapegoating (who goofed on the McGovern staff?)."

The Pentagon Papers story is another example of a major story that was the target of brickbats. On June 13, 1971, *The New York Times,* and subsequently other newspapers, published the papers of a secret Pentagon study of the Vietnam war. The government claimed the papers were stolen and filed charges against Dr. Daniel Ellsberg and Anthony J. Russo, Jr., who were accused of taking them. The charges were later dismissed but not before the government and administration supporters had flailed the press for printing the papers in the first place and distorting their significance in the second. At the outset of the Ellsberg-Russo theft trial, government prosecutors offered newspaper clippings which, they said, portrayed the defendants as "champions of a free press and a public and Congressional right-to-know; supporters of the Constitution; moral giants who performed acts of conscience at great personal risk and sacrifice; victims of racist attacks, government mistreatment and harassment; and courageous patriots whose only motive was to achieve peace." Judging by letters to newspapers around the nation, many readers agreed with the government's assessment. Earlier, the government had tried to suppress further circulation of the Pentagon Papers and succeeded by obtaining a federal court order halting publication. The ruling was later overturned by the United States Supreme Court on First Amendment grounds. It was the first time in U.S. history that the government had stopped publication of an article.

The Watergate bugging affair is still another instance of the public not always admiring press exposure. The furor was touched off after five men were arrested June 17, 1972, inside Democratic National Headquarters at the Watergate hotel-office complex in Washington, D.C. They apparently had planned to install listening devices on the premises and copy documents. Their seizure and subsequent conviction blossomed into one of the most far-reaching scandals in the history of this country. The President himself was accused of complicity in the bugging and several of his top staff members were known to have been involved.

The story made page one news throughout the land, but that failed to prevent many citizens from lashing out at the media for overplaying the episode and for alleged hostility toward President Nixon and the Republican Party. Man-in-the-street interviews in various parts of the country elicited such comments as, "The press is just trying to get Nixon," and "Why don't you guys [reporters] lay off Watergate?" Some persons appeared convinced that the entire Watergate matter was a media plot.

To these and other attacks, editors and publishers replied that Watergate, the Eagleton affair, and the Pentagon Papers incident were news, and big news at that. They said further that both reporters and editors made a conscientious effort to present the facts fairly and without bias. Moreover, the publishers correctly claimed that the great majority of newspapers had supported Nixon in his 1960, 1968, and 1972 election campaigns and therefore it was silly to accuse them of an anti-Nixon or anti-Republican disposition. As for the Eagleton business, the editors and publishers said it only proved that newspapers were not pushing for underdog McGovern, as some voters figured. And to top it all off, the newspapers asserted that the public had a right to be informed about all three events.

What conclusion can be sifted from all this? There are no absolute answers. Studies have shown that newspapers and other media are far more responsible than they were fifty or even twenty-five years ago. In 1952, the nation's newspapers were overwhelmingly bent toward the presidential election of Dwight D. Eisenhower over his opponent, Adlai Stevenson. When this was exposed in content analyses reports, the newspapers took note. When the same men ran again in 1956, the media leverage still favored Eisenhower but not by as much in *news* stories about the campaign. In the 1970s, newspapers and broadcast stations take special pains to give equal coverage to the major parties in a political race, regardless of their editorial position.

The individual reporter also is an important factor in whether a news story runs a straight or crooked line. Most newsmen and women strive for objectivity because that's the way they were taught and trained. But a reporter is not a robot programmed to dispense only unvarnished prose. He is a human being who sometimes is the victim of his background, experiences, religious and political beliefs, and his own conceptions in covering and writing a story. He may try to bury these elements but they can emerge despite his efforts. A reporter who had had a terrible time at prep school might unconsciously let his experiences color his story of the economic plight of private schools. One managing editor who was widely known and admired for his fearless crusading had this chink in his armor: He hated bookmakers and used his newspaper to campaign against them. These betting parlors violate the law in most states but the editor ran the issue to the ground. Any bookmaker's arrest, no matter how trivial, was emblazoned on page one, creating doubt as to whether the suspects could receive a fair trial. A reporter who is a war veteran is likely to tilt his story on veterans' benefits in behalf of a veterans' group. On the other hand, many metropolitan newsmen are members of the American Newspaper Guild, a trade union, and yet manage to write up labor-management disputes with complete objectivity. The point is that the possibility of personal preference creeping into a news article is always present. The journalistic profession does not deny this; it simply asserts that it doesn't happen often.

A Question of Accuracy

Almost every day, *The New York Times* features a boxed headline, "Correction," on the first page of its second section. Under the head are admissions of one or two goofs made by the newspaper the day before. Not all newspapers are that formalized in announcing errors, but they admit to them just the same.

Inaccuracies reflect on the credibility of a news medium just as much as bias or distortion. Actually, the latter failings are open to debate and interpretation. A newspaper or broadcast station can argue that the bias existed only in the eye of the beholder. Not so with clear-cut factual errors. There's nothing to debate when a wrong name is used or an untrue accusation made. There's nothing to interpret in a report that listed the sale of an office building at $300,000 when it should have been $3,000,000.

When one works for a newspaper, the importance of accuracy is drilled into one daily. One newspaper has signs posted around the city room reading: "Are Your Facts Right?" On most papers, consistent inaccuracy is a cause for dismissal and more than one reporter has lost his job that way. Editorial staffers are constantly admonished to check facts and then double-check them. Assume nothing, they are warned.

Yet mistakes happen—even on the best-managed newspapers and over the air. They happen because someone didn't check his facts carefully enough or took another person's word for a fact without verifying it. Errors also occur because reporters are usually in a hurry to meet deadlines and make slips in the process. Other inaccuracies are the result of wrong information given by sources, either deliberately or by honest error. There also is the typographical error, which is a printer's mistake and cannot be blamed on the reporter or editors. Daily newspapers with multiple editions usually catch most "typos" by the final edition.

Inaccuracies do more than damage a paper's or a station's image. They also lead to libel suits which can cost the news medium thousands of dollars—even millions—in judgments. Libel is contained in words which tend to expose a person to public hatred, shame, disgrace, or ridicule. A libel suit also may be brought by anyone who claims he was injured in his profession or business, such as a doctor who is called a "quack" in a news story. Certain words—thief, perjurer, communist, wife-beater, homosexual, deserter, etc.—are libelous on their face. The test is whether a person's reputation has been damaged. The strongest defense against libel is *provable truth.* A newspaper may print a seemingly libelous reference about an individual, knowing that it can prove the allegation. In other words, the news media sometimes take risks by knowingly publishing or broadcasting a libelous phrase or description. The law also permits the news media the right of *fair comment,* that is, they are entitled to provide certain information about a man, even though unflattering, if it is in the public interest. This right applies primarily to persons in public office. A newspaper, for example, may legally comment on the fact that a candidate for a judgeship lacks proper credentials for the post because he flunked out of three law schools before getting his degree at a fourth. Drama critics and sports writers are free to write disparagingly on the performance of actors or ball players under the fair comment rule.

The third libel defense is *privilege.* The law gives the news media the privilege of reporting the actions of judicial, legislative, and other public proceedings without incurring the danger of libel. This right covers the testimony of court witnesses, Congressional debates, and certain legislative and administrative hearings. Other statements and proceedings are deemed by the court to have *qualified privilege,* such as statements by police chiefs and other public officials.

When a libel is broadcast it is called *slander* and is subject to the same dangers. Libel becomes a criminal offense when it results in a breach of the peace. In this case, the action is brought by the district attorney and the penalty upon conviction could be a jail sentence or fine. Criminal libel is rare in the United States. In numerous other countries, it is used as a weapon for intimidating or shutting down newspapers which happen to disagree with government policy. This is unlikely to affect broadcast stations since they are owned and operated by the state in almost all foreign nations.

Editorial Policy

In Ansonia, Connecticut, a city teachers' group became so angry at the local newspaper that it urged readers to cease buying the daily or advertising in it. What drew their wrath was an editorial critical of a threatened job action by the teachers. According to the editor, the teachers admitted that the news articles about their action were fair and accurate. The editor added: "We believe the public has a right to know what is going on whether or not a particular group wants those facts known. As far as our editorial was concerned, we believe we have the right to present our considered opinions and intend to continue exercising that right without fear of reprisal."

The editor was on solid ground. The Constitutional guarantee of a free press gives newspapers the right to take any stand they desire. An editorial is an expression of a newspaper's feeling or opinion on a particular issue, whether it be war, peace, monetary policy, elections, the school system, or the price of corn. The traditional practice of American newspapers is to reserve a page or section of the paper for editorials so they will not be confused with news stories. Not all readers are aware of the difference. It is not uncommon for newspapers to be accused of bias on the basis of editorials, although their news accounts of the same issues may be perfectly objective. Insofar as editorials are concerned, newspapers can be as one-sided as they choose; that's the whole idea of an editorial.

Television and radio stations have adopted the same procedure by announcing to the listener in advance that what follows is an editorial statement by the station's management.

In cities where there is monopoly control of the media by a single ownership, the public suffers in being exposed to only one view. As part of their growing sense of responsibility, newspapers are conscious of this deficiency and attempt to leaven their editorial declarations with the opinions of outside columnists or guest editorial writers. Some conservative dailies like the *Oakland Tribune,* the *Chicago Tribune, The Kansas City Star,* and *The Detroit News* have opened their pages to liberal columnists. Similarly, liberal newspapers such as the *New York Post* feature right-leaning columnists such as William F. Buckley, Jr.

Sensationalism

American journalism is trying to live down its wild and woolly past. And a fairly recent past at that. Newspapers in this country were fairly well behaved up to the Civil War. The gusty circulation wars among the metropolitan dailies in the late nineteenth century changed all that. In their frenzied drive for a mass audience, newspaper tycoons such as Joseph Pulitzer, William Randolph Hearst, and James Gordon Bennett employed every sensational tactic they or their underlings could dream up. Pulitzer's New York *World* campaigned for readers' nickels and dimes to build a pedestal for the Statue of Liberty. Hearst was condemned for triggering the Spanish-American War by his *Journal*'s accounts of atrocities allegedly committed by Spanish soldiers in Cuba. The *World* sent Nellie Bly (real name, Elizabeth Seaman) dashing around the world in one of its more spectacular promotion stunts. The reporter was trying to beat the time of the hero of Jule's Verne's best-selling novel, *Around the World in Eighty Days*. She didn't make it. James Gordon Bennett, Jr., and his New York *Herald* made history when he assigned reporter Henry Morton Stanley in 1869 to find a lost explorer in Africa named David Livingstone. The mission was accomplished some two years later. The younger Bennett also created a news sensation in 1879 by financing the expedition of the ship *Jeanette* on a voyage to discover the North Pole. Unlike the Stanley expedition, this publicity caper did not meet with success. The vessel was crushed by polar ice and went down with all hands.

In the latter half of the 1800s, newspapers regularly ran such headlines as "Cut the Bookkeeper's Throat," "Killed the Girl Himself," and "Real American Monsters and Dragons," the last over an account of the unearthing of fossil remains of dinosaurs.

The raucous newspaper practices of the time led to the coining of the term "Yellow Journalism," which is still used by press critics. The phrase has nothing to do with cowardice. Its origin was in a *World* comic strip of that day called "Yellow Kid." The Kid was a poor street urchin who wore a long yellow nightgown which acquired its shade from the new color press installed by the newspaper. The cartoon quickly rose to popularity, attracting the attention of Hearst, who wanted it for his *Journal*. He tried to buy the cartoonist, Richard Outcault, away from the *World,* and the bitterness of the struggle between the publishers provided a handy label for everything that was wrong with American journalism.

There were some things right about these brawling newspapers of the 1880s and 1890s. For the most part, their editors and publishers were independent watchdogs of the public weal. They launched freeswinging crusades against municipal corruption, business trusts, and reeking slums. The same kind of journalism also flourished in the West, where the Chicago *Times* planted the headline, "Death's Debauch," over a story about a train wreck. But editors like William Rockhill Nelson of *The Kansas City Star* beat the drums for the public welfare and the *Denver Post* fought for legislation to wipe out child labor.

Circus newspapering continued into the twentieth century, becoming even more flamboyant in the 1920s jazz era and in the 1930s, when crime drove most other news off the front pages of the metropolitan dailies. Both decades produced a stream of stories about gangland killings, ax murders, bizarre sex crimes, and kidnappings. In 1934, hundreds of reporters converged on the little town of Flemington, New Jersey, for the trial of Bruno Richard Hauptmann, who was charged with the kidnapping and murder of the flyer-hero Charles Lindbergh's firstborn son. A few years earlier, the Hall-Mills murder case, whose victims were a preacher and a female church choir singer, had screamed out from newspapers across the country. This was the age of the tabloid, which came to be a synonym for sensationalism. Literally, the term means a newspaper folded to half size for easy reading on the subway.

American newspapers have sobered up considerably from their sensationalism binge, but that image lingers on. The conversion to a more staid makeup, the generally judicious use of blaring headlines, and the downplay of crime news cannot completely erase the idea that journalism is in bad taste. It can be argued, however, that sensationalism may be a state of mind. Momentous and horrifying events *have* taken place in the last fifteen years. A President; his brother, a Presidential candidate; and a noted black leader have been assassinated. Riots have torn apart our cities. Man has landed on the moon. The Vietnam war drove a President out of office and precipitated wide ruptures in our society. All these occurrences captured front pages and broadcast news programs. Were the media being sensational in reporting them in a prominent way? This is a difficult question to answer. There is no doubt these stories were news of great public interest. Should newspapers and other media withhold such items or give them low visibility?

If this should happen, many people would accuse the media of sinister secrecy.

One thing can be said with certainty. Most newspapers today do not go out of their way to foster sensationalism. Tastes have changed. Events which titillated readers in 1925 are considered laughable anachronisms today. How many people in this day and age would avidly follow the daily endurance of a flagpole sitter? Yet, this story commanded page one attention in the 1920s. We live now in a far more complex world than that of fifty years ago. Daily newspapers are replete with stories about the dollar crisis, food prices, civil rights, the environment, and foreign affairs. Even purely local issues are more complicated than they were twenty-five or fifty years ago.

Since the word "sensationalism" is closely linked to crime, let's examine that subject now.

Is Crime News Necessary?

A rather large segment of the media audience would probably answer this query in the negative. Some people seem to think that if crime isn't reported it doesn't happen or will go away. This is certainly not true in Boston, where the *Christian Science Monitor,* an otherwise distinguished newspaper, prints no crime stories.

Other questions that might be asked are: "Haven't the people the right to know about crime in their communities, in their neighborhoods? If a rapist is loose in a section of town, shouldn't residents be warned? If politicians are looting the public till, shouldn't the newspapers tell about it? If old women are being victimized by confidence games, shouldn't the word go out?"

One answer to these questions might be, "Yes, but. . . ." The "but" means that the media should report crime as a public service, but some newspapers, magazines, and broadcasters go too far in playing up murder and mayhem for their circulation value. Too much emphasis is put on gory details and criminals are often glamorized by the press, the critics contend. These charges are a little out of date. Crime news certainly has not disappeared from the media but its importance has greatly diminished in the minds of editors. Many newspapers are cutting back drastically on the number of crime articles, as compared with twenty-five years ago. The *New York Daily News,* the nation's leader in circulation, has reported a major reduction in police coverage and a sharper focus on urban affairs stories. Metropolitan editor John Smee noted that only the Manhattan and Brooklyn police beats are manned anymore as part of the tabloid's policy of sending highly qualified reporters "where the news is being generated."

"We're putting a lot of stress on housing, hospitals, welfare, and other city problems," he explained. "In the past, we took those matters too much for granted by making them general assignments."

The *Milwaukee Journal,* too, has swung away from crime toward urban affairs specialization in covering neighborhood organizations, slum rehabilitation, environment, and education. The Newark *Star-Ledger* eliminated the police beat entirely as a "wasteful process," according to editor Morton Pye. Police news is being handled by telephone from the city room, with reporters going out only on big stories.

"We found the police beat in Newark and the suburbs to be unnecessary," said Pye. "To justify their existence, police reporters were coming up with an enormous amount of trivia that was driving the city desk crazy. By having these reporters work out of the office, we are getting stronger police and municipal coverage."

Less emphasis on crime news has been similarly acknowledged by the *Chicago Tribune.* "Many routine police stories are now ignored," said city editor David E. Halversen. At the *Tribune* and other big-city dailies, attention is being shifted from standard police blotter items to news of organized crime. This trend has bred a reporter who is a crime specialist. He may spend weeks and months investigating syndicated criminal activities, police corruption, or the social effects of certain types of crimes such as mugging. *The New York Times* printed a revealing article about the indifference of New Yorkers to the murder of a woman whose screams for help they had heard. Other newspapers have elaborated upon the relationship of poverty to crime.

Actually, crime never has really dominated the newspapers. As early as 1900, Delos F. Williams reported in the *Annals of the American Academy of Political and Social Sciences* that his study of 240 newspapers revealed that only 3.1 percent of their contents was given over to crime news. In 1926, the Chicago *Evening American,* regarded as one of the most sensational in the Hearst chain, ordered a survey of several issues and found that only 6.3 percent of available space was devoted to crime. Dean Eric W. Allen, of the University of Oregon School of Journalism, directed a 1928 study of more than one hundred newspapers over a seventy-five-year span. Crime reports, he discovered, took up only 1.4 percent of the news allotment. By adding news of divorce and scandal, the figure was raised to 3.5 percent.

The proportion is even smaller today, although huge, black headlines about a major crime create a different impression for many readers. Television has added to this erroneous impression, despite the fact that its projection of crime stories statistically is far from overwhelming. Nonetheless, certain crime stories carry high visual excitement and are frequently selected for viewing by TV producers.

Finally, it must be stated that the media cannot be faulted for featuring some crime news. We live in a country with the highest crime rate in the world. There are obvious problems in our society which must be corrected. Censoring crime reports may only give citizens a false sense of security. It would not cure the ills that breed crime. Censorship, dictated or self-imposed, leads to more censorship. What would be censored after crime? Scandal? Military blunders? Drug usage? Benjamin Franklin, one of the nation's first newspapermen, neatly summed up the dilemma when he said: "If all printers were determined not to print anything till they were sure it would offend nobody, there would be very little printed."

Actually, studies have indicated a high reader interest in crime. A national survey by the American Newspaper Publishers Association in 1973 revealed that the most widely read news items were reports of accidents and disasters, crime, letters to the editor, and—among women—fashion and society stories. The study also showed that nearly half the average newspaper's pages are dominated by general news items.

Not Enough Local News

One characteristic of an item that is considered news is proximity. Generally, people are more interested in what happens in their community to persons they know. An old-time editor once remarked, "A dog-fight on Main Street is of more interest to our readers than fifty thousand foreign troops killed in battle somewhere." Media audiences are more sophisticated today, but local news still carries wide appeal.

Small-town papers are rarely scored for not publishing enough local news, this being their stock-in-trade. Some *are* blamed for lack of zeal in exposing civic wrongs or for not covering enough meetings and other affairs. Metropolitan editors, on the other hand, receive frequent complaints that their papers are overlooking vital community news in favor of national and international events. Neighborhood residents and groups have felt that large dailies are too impersonal, ignoring their needs and aspirations. Citizens of the Bay Ridge section of Brooklyn, of San Francisco's Sunset district, and of Chicago's "Back o' the Yards" area want to be represented in the daily press. Michael

Clendinin, city editor of the *New York Daily News,* told a journalism class: "We learned fast that people in Queens, Staten Island, and the Bronx really don't care very much about world affairs. What they want is news of their neighborhoods, their schools, their zoning problems and their tax rate."

In recent years, the *News* and other metropolitan dailies have paid closer attention to neighborhood events. Both the *News* and *The New York Times* have initiated neighborhood and suburban sections. Local coverage also has picked up in Chicago, Detroit, San Francisco, Cleveland, and many other cities. This is due partly to competition from television, to which millions turn for most or all of their news.

Minority groups and their members have one of the most legitimate grievances of all when they claim they are denied access to the news media. For years, blacks, Puerto Ricans, and Chicanos could get into the papers only by killing someone or committing other crimes. It took the bloody riots of the 1960s to bring home to the media what their neglect of minorities had cost the nation dearly. The situation has been corrected somewhat but there is a long way to go. Many blacks are still convinced that they are news only when their neighborhoods are in turmoil. The employment in the last few years of blacks and other minority members as reporters on newspapers has muted some of this criticism but the situation is far from resolved. Dailies in cities with large minority populations are printing more news about their ordinary lives and ambitions. The nationwide civil rights movement that began in the 1950s is another contributing factor to this change.

Not Enough National and International News

The protest that the media is too provincial comes mostly from better educated Americans. And they, too, have a point. For more than a century, the United States existed in a state of physical and cultural isolation from the rest of the world. The physical part couldn't be helped but the cultural withdrawal appeared to be a matter of preference, especially in the heartland. Even after World War I, Americans again wrapped themselves in isolationism. President Woodrow Wilson tried in vain to get this country into the League of Nations.

Much of this isolationism rubbed off on the press. The idea that things foreign were suspect persisted to the mid-twentieth century. It was only after World War II that the media became more global-minded, and not all of the media at that. To this day, many small-town newspapers print very few of the thousands of words of foreign news they receive on their AP and UPI machines. There are really only a few metropolitan dailies in the nation that offer a full portion of national and international news. In contrast, European newspapers tender their readers a generous helping of foreign news, particularly about the United States. This also is true of the larger dailies in Latin America. Foreign visitors to the U.S. are usually surprised at how little the American press has to say about the outside world.

It should be remembered that the mass media are just that. They aim at a mass audience, not at intellectuals. An individual who wants to be well informed on world affairs must go beyond his newspaper or television station. He is advised to supplement news reports by reading magazines such as *Harper's*, the *Atlantic Monthly, Time, Newsweek*, the *National Review, Foreign Affairs, U.S. News & World Report, The Nation*, the *New Republic*, and *Saturday Review/World*. In addition, a number of books deal with current events.

Some newspapers do provide a better-than-average sweep of national and foreign affairs. These include *The New York Times*, the *Washington Post*, the *Christian Science Monitor*, the *Chicago Daily News*, the *Los Angeles Times*, the *Louisville Courier-Journal*, and the *St. Louis Post-Dispatch*.

Too Much Bad News

In ancient days, the messenger who brought the king bad tidings not infrequently lost his head. The media, today's messenger, is often the focus of the same kind of wrath. Millions of people would prefer not to read or listen to bad news. When bad news takes the form of a seemingly endless story like the Vietnam war, Watergate, or rioting, there is a tendency to hold the press responsible. In the late 1960s, the media became the national scapegoat for racial rioting, crime, the Vietnam conflict, political assassinations, the New Left movement, and assorted other problems in our society. Animosity toward the press was shared by extremists on the left and right, black militants, white racists, law enforcement agencies, and a hefty portion of the intellectual community. During the 1968 Chicago Democratic Convention, a number of reporters and photographers were beaten by police on the streets. Governor George Wallace of Alabama was taking almost daily swipes at the "liberal, left-wing press" and a United States Senator proposed barring "news types" from the floor of presidential conventions. NBC announced that it had received 6,280 letters and telegrams—5,241 of them critical of the network's Chicago convention coverage.

Public reaction to the media has cooled somewhat in the 1970s. The *Washington Post* and other newspapers earned plaudits for exposing the Watergate mess and the Vietnam war did theoretically come to an end for the United States. Nevertheless, publishers and broadcasters always walk a tightrope in the matter of public opinion. The urge to blame someone else for news of wars, disasters, national embarrassments, and other unpleasantness is as American as apple pie. If no other whipping boy is around, the press will do nicely.

No sane person would argue that the media are faultless. But they do not create the bad news they report. They did not start the Vietnam war, burglarize

Watergate, or arouse the frustrations of blacks who had waited for two hundred years to share in the American dream. The newspapers do not send muggers into the streets, raise the price of beef, or cause the waters of the Ohio River to overflow its banks to destroy homes and people. These are all acts of man or nature.

There are occasions, however, when an overly flamboyant news account may exacerbate an already touchy situation. Untrained and irresponsible TV and radio newsmen undoubtedly inflamed the Newark race riots in 1967. A sloppily written story of a bread shortage may inspire a needless run on bakeries. An unduly optimistic report from the battlefield may raise false hopes of a truce or capitulation. People may dislike the press but they're prone to believe what they read and hear. Reporters and editors must assume a high standard of responsibility if they are to command confidence.

As for bad news, we can expect more of it. In an imperfect world, such tidings are as sure as sunrise. The only way to avoid them is to stop reading newspapers, watching television, and listening to the radio.

CHAPTER FIVE

Free Press and Fair Trial

Two Constitutional Amendments, the First and Sixth, had been on a collision course for nearly two hundred years. Minor collisions had occurred from time to time, but the big bang came in 1965, when the United States Supreme Court overturned the 1954 wife-murder conviction of Dr. Samuel Sheppard, an Ohio osteopath. In an eight-to-one decision, the court declared that he had been denied a fair trial because of the "virulent publicity" given the case by Cleveland newspapers and broadcast stations. A new trial was ordered and Dr. Sheppard was eventually freed.

The Constitutional issue implied by the case was clear. The First Amendment guarantees freedom of the press. The Sixth Amendment asserts that an accused person is entitled to a fair trial by an "impartial jury." Under our system, a person is presumed innocent until proved guilty.

The high court evidently believed that Sheppard had been convicted in the press before the jury ever brought in its verdict. There was substantial reason for the justices' conclusion. Prior to the osteopath's arrest, one Cleveland newspaper published editorials with such headlines as "Somebody Is Getting Away with Murder" and "Quit Stalling—Bring Him In." Before the trial began, newspapers and broadcast stations featured interviews with prospective witnesses, including Sheppard's girl friend. The Supreme Court said the trial itself was conducted in a "carnival atmosphere equivalent to bedlam." Reporters from all over the country appropriated most of the courtroom's seating capacity. During the trial, a local election was held in which both the judge and the chief prosecutor were candidates.

The Sheppard case issue was not new in America. As far back as 1878, a defendant in the Utah Territory petitioned the U.S. Supreme Court to reverse his bigamy conviction because the judge had seated jurors who admitted they had read about the case. In the 1930s, the dispute was reignited by the kidnapping of Colonel Charles Lindbergh's baby. Many lawyers and the American Bar Association expressed grave doubts as to whether the suspected kidnapper, Bruno Richard Hauptmann, received a fair trial in view of the blaze of publicity surrounding the crime.

The press won a victory in 1941, when the Supreme Court ruled that a judge cannot punish a journalist for contempt for commenting about a pending trial unless there is a "clear and present danger of obstructing justice." The Minnesota Supreme Court in 1963 upheld the 1963 conviction of St. Paul lawyer T. Eugene Thompson for plotting his wife's murder. The defense contended that he had been deprived of a fair trial because of media hoopla. The court conceded, however, that "It cannot be denied that the case was given an unusual amount of publicity, much of which could have been better omitted. The day may come when in this country we find a way to strike a fair balance between the Constitutional guarantee of a free press and the Constitutional right to a fair trial."

The question of pre-trial publicity and its potentially harmful effects also cropped up following the assassination of President John F. Kennedy in 1963. The Warren Commission Report rapped the press for its lack of discipline at Dallas and for publishing dozens of stories about the alleged killer, Lee Harvey Oswald, before he was to be tried. The trial was never held, of

AP

Reporters covering the Jack Ruby murder trial dash out the door of Judge J. Frank Wilson's courtroom in Dallas to flash to the world that Mrs. Louis Malone has been selected as the twelfth juror. Ruby was on trial for killing Lee Harvey Oswald, the man accused of assassinating President John F. Kennedy. The enormous publicity surrounding the slayings generated a heated free press vs. fair trial debate.

course. Oswald was himself assassinated as millions of horrified Americans watched on television.

The press denied that it acted improperly at Dallas. The media took the stand that the murder of a President is of such overwhelming importance that the facts must be brought to the public as quickly as possible. Reporters and editors also argued that the few instances of inaccurate reporting stemmed mainly from misinformation given by overexcited police at the scene. Dr. Wilbur Schramm, an eminent Stanford University mass communications expert, defended the press, writing:

The swift, full coverage [at Dallas] undoubtedly grounded many rumors before they could circulate. By speaking so fully and frankly of Oswald and the events in which he was involved, the media helped to reduce fears of a conspiracy and prepared people to believe the theory that a lone, disturbed man had done it. . . . For a student of communications, one of the most important deductions from the events . . . is that Americans trust their free press and their free broadcasting system. In this case, it must be said that these did not fail the American people in any important way. The people got the full news, they got it fast, and they got it, with few exceptions, accurately.

Neither the Kennedy assassination nor the Sheppard case resolved the fair trial/free press conflict. It would be a safe assumption that both intensified it. Following the Sheppard ruling, the American Bar Association named a committee to study the necessity of guidelines for lawyers, judges, prosecutors, and law enforcement officials in dealing with the press. The committee, headed by Associate Justice Paul C. Reardon of the Supreme Judicial Court of Massachusetts, came up with a series of strict recommendations to insure that criminal suspects get a fair trial. The proposals, which have been bitterly attacked by various sectors of the media, are generally advisory but they have gained wide acceptance in legal circles. Since the "Reardon Report,"

reporters have usually found it tougher to obtain pre-
trial information and, in some instances, have been
blocked from covering the trial itself. The South Bend
Tribune and other Indiana media went to court in
1973 to protest a county judge's ruling limiting press
coverage of his court. In recent years, two New York
judges have closed their courtrooms to both press and
public. A Pennsylvania judge imposed a sweeping gag
rule on all principals connected with the murder of
the operator of a home for retarded youths. In San
Francisco, however, a state appeals court in 1974 over-
ruled a judge who attempted to close off information
about the arrests of three men for allegedly committing
random street murders.

The Reardon strictures prohibit prosecutors and defense lawyers from giving the press such pre-trial facts
as the defendant's prior criminal record; confession
statements; results of any tests given the accused; the
identity, testimony, or credibility of prospective witnesses; the conjecture of a guilty plea; or any opinion
as to the suspect's guilt or innocence. However, law
officials may announce the fact and circumstances of
an arrest and the seizure of any physical evidence.
Similar rules of conduct are imposed on law enforcement officers but there is some question as to whether
a judge has authority over the police in the pre-trial
stage. At any rate, newsmen still find it easier to obtain
information from police and sheriff's officers than from
lawyers involved in a given case.

In one highly publicized crime case some observers
felt there was too much cooperation between police
and newsmen. On August 14, 1973, Houston police
dug up the twenty-seventh body of an undetermined
number of victims of a homosexual murder ring, making the killings the largest mass murder case in U.S.
history. As the facts of the bizarre crime unfolded
through the media around the nation, the Houston
district attorney reprimanded city homicide officers for
disclosing too many details to reporters. On the same
day, both the Houston *Chronicle* and the *Post* printed

verbatim on their front pages a handwritten, signed confession from an eighteen-year-old youth who was an alleged accomplice of the slayers. The DA claimed the disclosure of the confession would prejudice the suspect's eventual trial.

Doug Freelander, the *Post*'s city editor, claimed police had made copies of the confession available to all newsmen on the scene. "Personally," said Freelander, "I can't understand why the district attorney should take exception to the publication of the confession. This is not the first time it's happened. After all, this is a major crime story, and there is a certain amount of competition here. . . . Nobody's given us any specific reason why this information shouldn't be published."

The whole question of free press vs. fair trial hinges on whether or not prospective jurors are influenced in their decision-making by what they read or see in the media. It is virtually impossible in this society to avoid exposure to newspapers, magazines, television, or radio. But there is no way to look into a juror's mind to determine whether he has been influenced by what he has read or seen. Most say they have not been when questioned in the jury box. The law demands that the defendant's fate be decided solely on the basis of the evidence. Jurors are not supposed to come into the courtroom with their minds made up or even gravitating one way or another.

Studies of whether jurors' opinions are affected by the media are inconclusive.* For one thing, people do not like to admit to a prejudgment. The Supreme Court apparently thought the Sheppard trial jury absorbed too much media outpouring, but doubt continues. One of the most publicized cases in recent years was the burglary of the Los Angeles office of Dr.

---

* Two Columbia University social scientists reported in 1973 that their study showed that prejudicial trial publicity influences juries and affects their verdicts. According to their findings, jurors exposed to prejudicial news stories were as much as 66 percent more likely to find defendants guilty than were jurors who read only "straight" news reports.

Daniel Ellsberg's psychiatrist. Ellsberg was charged with stealing the notorious Pentagon Papers. The office break-in was carried out by two White House staff members, it was later learned. Yet, most prospective grand jurors interviewed in the burglary proceedings said they had not read about the Ellsberg and Pentagon Papers cases. Their response was reasonable. Millions of newspaper readers are headline skimmers, and do not take note of every headline. Relatively few persons wade through an entire story, especially if it is long and involved. Also pertinent is the fact that people forget. Today's page one news has slipped from memory a week or two later. It is logical to assume that a man called to jury duty six months or a year after the defendant's arrest is unlikely to have retained a clear impression of what he had read, seen, or heard about the case.

The First vs. Sixth Amendment controversy is obscured by a number of other factors. For one thing, most suspects plead guilty, thus eliminating the need for a trial. Also, most crimes are of such a routine nature that they receive little or no publicity. In most instances, a jury venireman can say quite truthfully that he had never heard of the person on trial or his alleged crime. It is usually only the sensational case that brings the issue into question. Trials like those of Hauptmann, Sheppard, and an Oswald stir up the coals of this conflict. Still, it would be tragic if even one person were executed or sent to prison because of pre-trial news coverage. Should action be taken to prevent such a miscarriage of justice? If so, what kind of action should it be and who should be granted authority to take it? Many lawyers feel that the right of fair trial is more important than the right of the press to gather and report the news. The news media contend that a democratic society cannot exist without a press free of restraints. Newsmen assert further that pre-trial investigative reporting has led to the release of innocent persons accused of crimes. One case cited is that of George Whitmore, Jr., a youth arrested for the brutal murder of two young women in their New York apartment. Police gave out Whitmore's alleged confession and the press printed it. Then reporters began digging and located witnesses who could furnish an alibi for the suspect, who was eventually cleared of the charge. The youth was later convicted of another crime, sentenced to prison, and freed several years later, the victim again of an apparent miscarriage of justice.

The press also maintains that police bungling or skulduggery cannot be hidden if their investigations come under reporters' surveillance. And officers are less inclined to procrastination in their probe if the press is on their heels, newsmen claim. These justifications bear some merit, but sometimes the police, under press harassment, are too quick to "solve" a crime. They produce a suspect who is freed a few days later, completely cleared of the felony. However, the use of his name and picture in the media may have harmed his reputation and embarrassed his family. No innocent person should be sacrificed to the demands of a news medium, ambitious police chief, or district attorney. The press and the law must work together to protect the rights of individuals.

Much pre-trial information is generated by self-serving prosecutors hoping to ride to political stardom on the case. They stage press conferences at which they bring out confessions and freely discuss the crime. Lawyers play the same game in trying to create a favorable climate of opinion for their clients, whom they make readily available to reporters. The author can recall one obliging attorney who went into his client's jail cell with a small tape recorder concealed in his coat. Later, he played the tape of the accused's remarks to newsmen who had been alerted to the move.

Since the adoption of the Reardon Report by the American Bar Association, judges have shown a marked tendency not only to snuff out pre-trial coverage but to bar reporters from the trials themselves. In Brooklyn, New York, Federal Judge John R. Bartels ordered a *Daily News* reporter not to publish material regarding the prior criminal record of a labor leader on trial for extortion. When the newspaper's attorney argued against the ruling, the judge replied: "I certainly am not trying in the least to interfere with freedom of the press. I'm pleading for fairness. I'm all for freedom of the press but I am also insistent that this man get a fair trial."

The judge had objected to a statement printed by all three New York newspapers, terming it a "blatant, flagrant, and intentional attempt to prevent a fair trial." The statement alleged the defendant "had long been a target of local and federal law enforcement authorities and had figured prominently in a newspaper series on organized crime at Kennedy Airport."

Alexander Greenfield, a *New York Times* attorney, retorted that the jurors, having taken an oath not to discuss the case among themselves or read about it in news reports, could not be prejudiced by any news stories. The accused's lawyer sought a mistrial on the strength of the articles, but Judge Bartels denied it.

A few months later, Judge Bartels declared a mistrial in another case after accusing the *Times* and the *Daily News* of prejudicing the jury in the trial of reputed mob figures charged with harboring a murder suspect. Before selection of the jury began, the judge called reporters before the bench and said: "Please use restraint. And if any of these defendants [there were four in all] have any prior record, please do not publish it."

Both newspapers, however, printed stories revealing the defendant's criminal records. The editors declared that the public was entitled to read about the trial in the context of its public significance.

The next day, Judge Bartels asked the jurors if they had read either article. Two said they had and two others said they had been told about the stories.

A *Times* spokesman explained: "Certain facts were considered essential to the reader's understanding of the story and trial. Our position has always been to accommodate the rights of fair trial with those of the free press and, indeed, the *Times* has been particularly sensitive to these issues. Under the First Amendment, the decision as to what a newspaper will print about a trial . . . must rest with the newspaper in accordance with responsible journalistic standards."

The *News* representative said: "The *News* policy is to give a fair break to everybody in court. It is also to give the public a fair share of what goes on in the world, including the courtroom. Reporting the background of a defendant informs the public of the significance of the case."

In granting the mistrial sought by defense attorneys, Judge Bartels commented: "This is due to the failure of the press to make every effort to grant these defendants a fair trial." He then discharged the jury and announced that he would try the case himself. It was a classic example of a First and Sixth Amendment conflict.

An equally crucial conflict erupted between the courts and two Baton Rouge, Louisiana, newspapermen. Late in 1973, the Supreme Court refused to hear an appeal of contempt citations against Larry Dickinson of the *State-Times* and Gibbs Adams of the *Morning Advocate*. Both had published accounts of an open federal court hearing in defiance of a court order. A U.S. district judge had fined the two newsmen three hundred dollars each when they ignored his directive not to write about a conspiracy case against a local civil rights leader. The Reporters' Committee on Freedom of the Press said that the Supreme Court's refusal to hear the appeal "means that any judge can order a newspaper not to publish any news item, and the newspaper must obey that gag for as long as it takes to appeal. By that time, the item may no longer be newsworthy."

In 1973 Circuit Judge Tom Huff, of Plymouth, Indiana, refused to allow open coverage of a murder trial, despite the threat of legal action against him. He ruled that only one reporter could cover the trial and then supply his notes to other newsmen waiting outside. Indiana law requires all courts to be open.

In San Bernardino, California, Judge Don A. Turner took testimony in 1972 in a prostitution case behind closed doors, releasing the text later to the press. The procedure was protested by the local chapter of Sigma Delta Chi, the professional journalistic society.

"We had no idea of what was being said in that secret testimony," said Chapter President Carl Yetzer. "Some of it might have been important for the people of San Bernardino."

One judge who barred reporters from a New York conspiracy trial was slapped down by the State Court of Appeals in 1972, which ruled he had trampled on the First Amendment's guarantee against censorship. Before closing the trial, Judge George Postel had warned newspapers about printing information about the defendant's criminal record. At one point, he threatened to put reporters "in the can" for defying his orders. The Appellate Court said that Postel's dictum "could not help but have a deterrent effect on free discussion by the press."

Many judges and lawyers feel that the press should voluntarily abide by the Reardon Report restrictions. Just as many newsmen and publishers heatedly resist the suggestion. Sam Boyle, a Philadelphia *Bulletin* editor, put it this way: "I don't even like the word 'guidelines' because that implies something that you're going to follow. I consider them dangerous because they limit the right of the public to know, and I think the public has the right to know what is going on in the community. The Bar Association doesn't want us to publish criminal records of men arrested for crimes. I think the public should know who is the suspect in a crime. If he's an editor, fine; if he's a radio announcer, fine. If he happens to be a man with a record of ten arrests, I think that's an essential part of the story, too."

Washington Star-News editor Newbold Noyes, Jr., said: "Yes, we want fair courts, where the accused gets a fair break. But we also want a citizenry which is keenly aware of the magnitude of the crime problem confronting these courts, and of exactly how that problem is—and isn't—being met."

After the Watergate story broke, questions were raised as to whether the principals in the case could receive a fair trial if they were indicted. The case, which was widely aired in newspapers and on television and radio, involved a score of one-time White-House and administration leaders. Speculation was also broached that, even if the defendants were found guilty, the convictions would be reversed by an appeals court on the grounds that the accused persons had been bathed in such a glare of publicity that an impartial jury was impossible to find. The same problem was presented for former Vice-President Spiro T. Agnew, who was mentioned in connection with a criminal investigation in Baltimore, Maryland. *The New York Times,* which had criticized Agnew editorially in the past, said of the investigation: "Like every other citizen, Mr. Agnew is entitled to the presumption of innocence while that scrutiny goes on. Judgment has to be reserved until all the facts are known. Only when and if an indictment is returned would there be need to consider Agnew's appropriate role pending ultimate determination of his guilt or innocence. . . ."

The *Times* soon found itself directly involved in the Agnew investigation. In 1973 the Vice-President's lawyers served at least seven subpoenas on news organizations and reporters, including a *Times* man, in a search for news leaks from the Justice Department about the case.

The subpoenas had been authorized by Federal Judge Walter E. Hoffman after Agnew's attorneys had complained that premature disclosures from government investigators had made it impossible for a grand jury to consider fairly and objectively the allegations against the Vice-President. The investigation concerned reported illegal kickbacks Agnew had received from

Maryland contractors while he was governor of that state.

Agnew charged that the alleged leaks from the Justice Department were "malicious, immoral and illegal." In handing down his order for the subpoenas, Judge Hoffman indicated grave misgivings about the role of the press in disseminating the leaked information. "We are rapidly approaching the day," he said, "when the perpetual conflict between the news media, operating as they do under freedom of speech and freedom of the press, and the judicial system, charged with protecting the rights of persons under investigation for criminal acts, must be resolved."

The subpoenas became moot when Agnew resigned the Vice-Presidency and pleaded no contest to a tax evasion charge.

The news media quickly made it clear that, in their view, subpoenaing reporters was not an acceptable way of resolving the issue. The subpoenas had been protested by all the organizations receiving them. In addition to the *Times,* the orders were served on representatives of the *Washington Post,* the *New York Daily News,* the *Washington Star-News, Newsweek,* CBS, and *Time.* All opposed the subpoenas on First Amendment grounds.

A *Times* spokesman said: "This attempt to force disclosure of confidential sources and information is a violation of the First Amendment. Unless reporters can use information from persons not in a position to have their names revealed, investigative reporting will be eliminated. Without investigative reporting, the press will not be able to look beneath the surface of the news and the purpose and function of a free press will be severely damaged."

Time Inc. stated: "We believe that confidentiality of sources is essential to the gathering of news." Joseph A. Califano, attorney for the *Washington Post* and *Newsweek,* which are jointly owned, declared: "We consider these subpoenas an invasion of our rights under the First Amendment, particularly since any response to them would require the revelation of confidential sources."

There are signs that some newspapers are at least willing to discuss the free press/fair trial problem with the legal profession. In New York, lawyers, judges, and newsmen formed a committee to study the issue and possibly arrive at a compromise. The group was headed by former State Supreme Court Judge Bernard Meyer, who had been a member of the Reardon Committee. Missouri journalists and lawyers have also initiated a dialogue to foster better understanding and cooperation between the press and the bar. At their first meeting, the delegates were surprised at the extent to which both sides agreed on free press/fair trial and other issues. Similar meetings have been held in other states.

Some observers of the debate believe this country should adopt the English system of pre-trial reporting. The rule there is that any act deemed to interfere with "due course of justice" will bring contempt charges against the doer. British journalists must tread far more lightly in pre-trial coverage than their American counterparts. Stiff jail sentences have been handed out to English reporters who had broken the rule. A British newspaper may be held in contempt if it comments on any pre-trial proceedings, including the arrest of a suspect. A Scottish newspaper company was fined heavily for reporting that a man was merely detained by police for questioning about two murders. American editors say the English system cannot work here for several reasons. One is that it would violate the Constitutional guarantee of a free press. A second is that British cases are tried more quickly than in the United States, where most courts have a huge backlog. A third reason is that American reporters would never stand for it.

The British press is not as sedate as its pre-trial rules might imply. Several of the mass circulation London dailies are sensational to a degree that is not often encountered in the United States. Aside from pre-trial publicity, English newspapers are quite free to print anything they choose. The popular press there has had a field day with sex scandals involving prominent government figures.

One possible solution to the free press/fair trial imbroglio is pool coverage of major trials. This system is already used in covering certain stories. Under the pool arrangement, one reporter and possibly a photographer representing several media are given access to the news source. Later, their notes and pictures are shared with their competitors. Thus, all the media carry substantially the same account of the event or interview. The President of the United States has imposed this method on coverage of a White House affair or meeting by inviting a single cameraman from the Associated Press or United Press International to take pictures. The photos are then distributed to the press at large. The advantage of the pool with big stories is that it allows for an orderly coverage of the event.

The pool idea has serious drawbacks, however. One is that reporters like to ask their own questions and pursue a story in their individual ways. In the case of a court trial, two reporters might differ on the importance of testimony or the composure of a witness. The pool also makes for a bland uniformity in the news and cuts down the flow of information to the public. Another danger is that it makes it easier for the news source to control or manipulate the news to his own advantage.

Before a final solution can be found to the fair trial/free press difference, answers must be found to these crucial questions: What exactly is prejudicial publicity? Are people really influenced by what they read in the newspapers or hear on the radio and TV? Is it possible for a juror to go into a trial with a preconceived notion but change his mind when he hears the evidence? How much do jurors retain of what they have read or heard about a case? Is the public getting a fair shake if the media are hamstrung in telling the facts about a crime and subsequent arrests?

Both the news media and the bar must share responsibility for any injury to a defendant that might
spring from pre-trial reporting. The ideal goal is the
absolute assurance of a fair trial while acknowledging
the public's right to know.

CHAPTER SIX

The Media and Government

FEW IN THE media were surprised to learn that a White House "enemies list," revealed at the Watergate hearings, contained the names of many prominent newsmen. Among those singled out were Daniel Schorr, CBS-TV news reporter; syndicated columnists Jack Anderson, Marquis Childs, and Mary McGrory; former NBC anchorman Chet Huntley; *New York Times* executives and columnists James Reston and Tom Wicker; *Newsday* senior editor Robert Greene; Edwin O. Guthman, national editor of the *Los Angeles Times;* and James Deakin, *St. Louis Post-Dispatch* White House correspondent. They and the numerous other journalists on the list had one thing in common: They had written or broadcast stories the Nixon administration had considered unfriendly.

The White House did more than make lists. Schorr was the subject of an FBI investigation for several weeks. Greene's tax returns were audited after he had directed a *Newsday* team investigation of the financial affairs of Charles (Bebe) G. Rebozo, a close friend of President Nixon. The acting FBI director admitted at a May, 1973, news conference that the bureau had tapped the telephones of four newsmen to determine responsibility for leaks of "highly sensitive and classified information." *Washington Post* reporters were excluded from covering certain White House functions.

Many Washington newsmen had criticized Nixon as being the most inaccessible President in recent history, holding press conferences months apart. During the Watergate affair, the President remained unavailable for several weeks at a time. Journalists also accused the chief executive of harboring a long-standing animosity toward them, a fact which the administration found hard to deny. Richard M. Nixon had been at odds with the press since he first entered politics in the 1940s. In 1962, when he lost the California gubernatorial election, he told assembled reporters, in bitterness: "Well, you won't have Nixon to kick around anymore."

Prophecy failed. The future President was going to be around for many years, to the dismay of some reporters, if not their publishers. One week before the 1972 Presidential election, Nixon had the editorial support of 71.4 percent of the 1,054 daily newspapers participating in an *Editor & Publisher* Magazine poll. Newspaper editorials and coverage also were largely pro-Nixon in 1968. The heavy margin may have played a significant role in his narrow victory that year, according to a study by the University of Michigan Institute for Social Research. The findings showed that the Democratic candidate, Senator Hubert Humphrey, got a better break from television.

Still, it is the working reporters and columnists with whom a President must deal on a daily basis. There is the feeling in the Nixon administration that a large number—if not most—of the newsmen and women who cover the White House range from liberal to left-wing in their political thinking. This state of mind, according to the theory, produces advocacy journalism unfavorable to the White House.

"We have some dangers in many ways in the profession of journalism," Herbert G. Klein, President Nixon's former communications director, warned in a *New York Times* article. "I happen to be one who does not believe reporters should be advocates. I think that their job is to report, to interpret the background."

Other administration supporters have been more

direct in their slaps at the media. Senator Barry Gold-water, of Arizona, who often takes the White House side in its differences with the press, declared in a 1973 *Newsday* article that "For four years, he [Nixon] has been the victim of the most vicious personal attacks. Day and night, America's predominantly liberal national media hammered at Mr. Nixon, slicing from all sides, attacking, hitting, and cutting. . . ."

James Keogh, former special assistant to Nixon, roasted the media in his book *President Nixon and the Press.* The author, a reporter and editor for thirty years, accused his former colleagues of inadequate reporting and of letting their personal prejudices influence their stories. For this reason, Keogh wrote, Nixon preferred to bypass the White House correspondents and talk directly to the people over television. He quoted the President as saying that "Without television it might have been difficult for me to get people to understand a thing about Southeast Asia."

John D. Ehrlichman, Nixon's domestic affairs assistant until the Watergate incident dislodged him from office, attributed the dearth of Presidential press conferences to the "flabby and fairly dumb questions" asked by reporters. He compared the newsmen to "insecure young ladies who keep asking if we still love them. Then, when we tell the truth, there is a hurt feeling that sets in."

Editor & Publisher Magazine (June 24, 1972) retorted that the charge was "unfounded and phony and seems like just another attempt to discredit the press corps." The magazine then listed twenty-one "hard" questions asked Nixon at a single news conference, describing them as relating to current and important news developments.

Newsmen, for their own part, have accused the Nixon administration of creating a climate of suspicion and hostility against them. Daniel Schorr told the Senate Constitutional Rights Committee that the White House-ordered FBI investigation of him had a "chilling" effect on all newsmen. "Anyone concerned about freedom of the press," he added, "must be concerned about the climate of fear the administration has helped to create." Schorr said he sensed a "concerted" attempt to discredit the news media. Other newsmen on the list also expressed deep resentment. Ted Knap, a Scripps-Howard reporter, took his listing with a grain of humor. Writing in his company's internal magazine, Knap asked:

How did a nice guy like me get on the White House enemies list? It was an undeserved honor, or, as the head tenant would say, a bum rap.

Before Watergate, which came after the "enemies" list was compiled, I had a high regard for Richard M. Nixon as a public official and as a politician. In covering him occasionally since 1950 and intensively since 1966, I firmly believe that I have been fair and objective, and that by any reasonable standard he made out OK in the cumulative total of what I had written about him pre-Watergate.

So I was flabbergasted to learn that I had made the list.

My first thought was that Pat Buchanan, White House speech writer and media critic, must have had something to do with compiling the list. Sure enough he was one of the four who, according to the testimony of former White House counsel John W. Dean, III, contributed names to the list.

It is Buchanan's view that if you are not for Nixon, you are against him. We have exchanged sharp differences of opinion on this. . . .

Buchanan, one of the President's more acerbic press critics, suggested in 1972 that the Nixon administration consider antitrust legislation against the three big television networks for what he termed their "monopoly" on news presentation. Referring to the networks' "liberal bias," he said over the educational television network that if the major TV networks continue to "freeze out opposing points of view and opposing information, you're going to find something done in the area of antitrust type action." The White House later

UPI

UPI White House Chief Helen Thomas (left) is on the scene with President Nixon as he leaves Constitution Hall following a concert.

announced that Buchanan was speaking for himself alone.

The swords-point relationship of Mr. Nixon and the press is not new in the history of this nation. An adversary association has existed between the White House and newsmen since George Washington's day. The father of this country received more than his fair share of press criticism which, no doubt, accounted for his distaste for newspapers and the men who wrote for them. Washington's attitude toward the press was reflected in an incident during the 1787 Constitutional Convention in Philadelphia. A copy of the proposals, which had been mislaid by a delegate, was found and turned over to Washington, the convention president. As the meeting was adjourning for the day, the Revolutionary War hero asked the members to remain seated a few minutes longer. Then, displaying the lost copy and eyeing the group sternly, Washington said:

"Gentlemen, I am sorry to find that some one member of this body has been so neglectful of the secrets of this convention as to drop in the State House a copy of their proceedings which, by accident, was picked up and delivered to me this morning. I must entreat, gentlemen, to be more careful, lest our transactions get into the newspapers and disturb public response by premature speculations."

At the end of Washington's second term, Thomas Jefferson wrote James Madison: "Little lingering fevers have been hanging around him [Washington] a week or ten days. He is also extremely affected by the attacks made & kept upon him in the public papers. I think he feels these things more than any person I ever yet met with. . . ."

Jefferson himself had his own troubles with the press as President. He got back at his critics by using the newspaper the *National Intelligencer* as a spokesman for his administration. His enemies promptly accused him of news management but he denied using the *Intelligencer* for personal power. He could not be blamed much if he had. At least four other newspapers kept up a constant barrage against the President and his staff. This was the era of the party press, when journalism was as much an instrument for propaganda as for news. Nonetheless, history records Jefferson as a defender of the press.

Nor was Jefferson the last President to be the target of press broadsides. Zachary Taylor got a bad press throughout his administration, as did Franklin Pierce. Opposition papers called Taylor "an ignorant tyrant," a "butcher," and a "whitened sepulchre." Pierce, growing weary of the brickbats hurled at him, assigned his secretary to screen the newspapers, giving him only such items as he thought the President ought to hear. This practice, with some refinements, continues to this day.

Abraham Lincoln got along well with the press most of the time, but even his easygoing nature could shift suddenly to rage. One day he stormed into the office of U.S. Treasurer L. E. Chittenden, waving a news clipping and shouting violently. A New York newspaper had accused him of drawing his salary in gold while Union soldiers were being paid in greenbacks worth only fifty cents on the dollar. "I hope the scoundrel who wrote this will boil hereafter," he told Chittenden. Lincoln's principal problem with the press during the Civil War was censorship. Correspondents chafed under the restrictions then imposed, and Lincoln frequently found himself in the middle between the irate newsmen and his army commanders and cabinet officers, who had issued the orders withholding certain information. General William Tecumseh Sherman threatened to hang one correspondent for reporting his defeat at Vicksburg. The reporter was actually tried as a spy for the South, but a board of officers merely ordered him out of the war zone.

Grover Cleveland, a sedate, grave man, started his relations with the press on a particularly sour note. A bachelor most of his life, he surprised the nation by marrying a young and attractive girl during his Presidency. The wedding was held in Washington under close secrecy and the couple slipped away to a honeymoon in Maryland. The press tracked them down, however, putting their cottage retreat under a virtual state of siege. When the pair stepped out on the porch for a breath of evening air, reporters raced to the telegraph office to report the event. Finally, giving full vent to his feelings, Cleveland referred to the horde of reporters as "newspaper nuisances" and "animals." The situation did not improve. President Cleveland developed a near paranoia about being followed about by the press on his trips, calling it a "pestilence." Once, as he was about to address a gathering at Harvard University, he departed from his text just long enough to deliver a few scalding remarks toward the row of reporters covering the speech.

President Theodore Roosevelt generally tolerated the newspapers, shrewdly using them to advance his ideas and programs. An exception was made for re-

porters bold enough to disagree with him or otherwise
ruffle his feathers. These unfortunates were banished to
his self-styled "Ananias Club," named after the Biblical
liar who fell dead when Peter rebuked him. TR also
had no hesitation in phoning an editor to demand that
he fire a reporter who had written something that
displeased him. That practice has not gone out of
style, either. But Presidents with this request learn
quickly that editors reserve completely the right to
discharge staffers in their own good time and for their
own reasons.

Presidential infighting with the press continued into
modern times. Warren G. Harding, who came to the
Presidency following a career as an Ohio newspaper
publisher, thought he would have no problem in getting
along with newsmen. "I know all about reporters," he
told friends. "They will not let me down." A year later
he thought that they had. Harding, whose geniality
cloaked a limited intellectual capacity, committed a
series of foot-in-mouth blunders that were faithfully
reported, much to his discomfort. The climax came one
day during a speech at the National Press Club, where
he declared, "I do not regard the four-power Pacific
pact as covering the principal islands claimed by Japan." When this was printed the next day, diplomatic
sparks flew over the world. Besides, the comment went
contrary to the position of Harding's own secretary of
state, who offered his resignation. The President looked
for a handy scapegoat and found it in the press. He
directed that all news questions be presented to him in
writing, and answered only those he chose. When the
famed Teapot Dome scandal flared up (it was the
Watergate of its day), the last vestiges of goodwill
between Harding and the press vanished. His press
secretary bluntly told reporters at one point that he
expected favorable publicity for Harding or none at
all. The request, to say the least, was not granted.

A taciturn, aloof man at best, Herbert Hoover remained at arms-length distance from the press during
almost his entire four years as President. The Great

Depression, which threw the nation into the economic doldrums, did not help Hoover's image with the country or the White House correspondents. The latter did not blame the President for the downturn, only for avoiding questions about it.

Franklin Delano Roosevelt was the first President to put his relations with the press on a formal, regular basis. He initiated twice-weekly press conferences, inviting reporters to let the questions fly. The newsmen, forced for years to endure Presidents Coolidge and Hoover's written-question order, took Roosevelt at his word. The President seemed to enjoy the exchange as he leaned back expansively, a cigarette holder jutting rakishly up from his teeth. FDR's romance with the press did not extend to publishers, most of whom opposed him until the day he died at the beginning of his fourth term. When Roosevelt felt that the news play was running against him he blamed the newspaper owners, rather than the reporters. The President's New Deal policies came under constant attack in editorials, and some newspapers charged him with provoking the war with Japan.

Harry Truman, who began his Presidency with some timidity toward publicity and the press, wound up on a smooth footing with the White House newsmen, who liked his homespun, straightforward style. They didn't find him as voluble as Roosevelt, but few Presidents in history have been.

Dwight D. Eisenhower was the first President who had to deal on a broad scale with television as well as the print press. To aid him, he had one of the best secretaries in modern times, James Hagerty, who also was one of the President's closest advisers. Hagerty, a former newsman, was an expert in grabbing headlines and skillfully keeping the press at bay with regular news tidbits—even when Ike was on the golf course. When Eisenhower met the press at televised and office press conferences, he was amiable and relaxed, thanks to Hagerty's coaching. His dander could be raised quickly, though, if he took a reporter's question as hostile or embarrassing. At one conference, angered by the frequency of sharp queries on the assaults made on his administration by Senator Joseph McCarthy, Eisenhower angrily strode from the room.

A reasonably peaceful relationship between the White House and the press corps continued through the Kennedy administration, although the President was sometimes criticized for attempting to manipulate the news and for playing favorites among certain reporters by granting them exclusive interviews. JFK could become quite chilly when questions were raised about problems in his administration. If reporters probed too deeply during news conferences, Kennedy neatly sidestepped the question, forcing the newsmen and women to go on to something else. During crisis periods, Kennedy would put off press conferences for weeks at a time. At one point he canceled the White House subscription to the *New York Herald Tribune,* which he thought was being unfair to his administration.

Midway in his term, Kennedy was asked about White House press coverage. "Well," he answered, "I am reading more and enjoying it less—but I have not complained, nor do I plan to make any general complaints. I read and talk to myself about it, but I don't plan to issue any general critical statement of the press. They are doing their task . . . and I am attempting to do mine, and we are going to live together for a period of time and then go our separate ways."

The antagonisms that exist now between the White House and the press are rooted in the administration of Lyndon Baines Johnson. President Johnson, to begin with, was a secretive man. Also, the Vietnam war developed into a major struggle during his years in office, splitting the nation and forcing the administration into a defensive posture. The terms "credibility gap" and "news management" came into full flower during the Johnson era. In the first few months of his term, press relations had deteriorated to a low point and remained there. White House correspondents com-

plained about Johnson's passion for secrecy, his in-
formationless press conferences, his extreme sensitivity
to criticism, his misunderstanding of the press's role,
and his inclination to outright deception.

President Johnson, the newsmen added, expected
the press to be a cheerleader for the Presidency. This
is unreasonable in a democratic society with a free
press, they noted. Pierre Salinger, who served LBJ
briefly as press secretary after the death of his first
boss, John F. Kennedy, said that Johnson regarded the
secretaryship as a "propaganda tool."

"To him," Salinger continued, "the job was self-
serving. I believed, on the other hand, that propaganda, to be effective, must be candid. The relationship
between the President and the press breaks down when
a one-hundred-percent effort is made to get the press to
write praise stories about the President. LBJ had no
real concept of the role of the press as observer and
critic. I always looked at the press as friendly enemies
—to hope for the best and expect the worst."

To some observers—mostly on the media side—the
gulf between the government and the press is not entirely
a bad thing. They contend that when a too cozy
rapport obtains between reporters and officials there is
less likelihood of hard-hitting, let-the-chips-fall-where-
they-may reporting. Newsmen would be reluctant to
write uncomplimentary stories about their friends, according to this theory. Most journalists would readily
admit the basic truth of this viewpoint. It is no accident when Presidents turn to "friendly" reporters
when they want to leak an important plan or idea to
the public. They and other government officers do not
hesitate to use the press for their ends if the opportunity arises. James McCartney, national correspondent
in Washington for the Knight Newspapers, candidly
explained the practice in the winter 1969–70 issue of
the *Columbia Journalism Review* article:

The press is often used. The federal government is so
accustomed to using it for its own ends that presidents

become annoyed and irritable when they find, to their surprise, that on some occasions they cannot do so. This is the context in which Vice President Spiro Agnew's remarks about the news media belong. Agnew was frustrated and angry because some analysts and commentators criticized President Nixon's November 3 speech on Vietnam. Agnew had nothing to say about the fact that day after day, week in and week out, most White House ploys designed to build a favorable image of the president and his administration are dumped undigested on a public which often does not have sufficient time or information to evaluate them on its own.

The immense prestige of the U.S. presidency today leads the media to make a giant of any man who holds the job, regardless of his personal limitations. The most innocuous statement from President Nixon is often treated as though it were a pronouncement of intrinsic worth from on high. . . .

This is all very well when the government *wants* to give out news. When the opposite is true, the problem for the press becomes one of access, a key factor in strained relations between media and government. There are numerous occasions when a President or other official doesn't want certain matters known to the public. A pattern of secrecy is established which sometimes includes lying to reporters. During the Eisenhower administration, the government lied about the fact that a U-2 spy plane had been shot down over Russia. The truth came out when the Soviets showed pictures of the wrecked plane and the captured pilot. More recently, the White House and the Pentagon conspired to conceal air raids into Cambodia while this country was publicly affirming that such attacks were prohibited for U.S. aircraft. The Watergate hearings revealed numerous instances of official deception.

The media take the position that they act in the public's interest. Even if the government lies, they claim, it is the reporter's job to sniff out the truth and expose it, regardless of how irritating this is to the

President or anyone else. This, of course, is the concept on which a free press is based—the public's right to know. Newspapers and broadcast stations which backed off a story every time the government raised its hand would have little to be proud of. The journalist must pursue his leads wherever they take him, regardless of official displeasure.

But is there a time when the government is justified in withholding news or lying? Yes, in a legitimate case of national security, a term frequently invoked by officials defending secrecy. The news corps recognize this as a valid reason. Media owners and employees regard themselves as just as patriotic as anyone else. They will, at the drop of a hat, recite their undisputed wartime record of not publishing or broadcasting anything that might have aided the enemy. There is, however, an understandable reluctance by reporters to believe officials every time they raise the banner of national defense. Time and again, the government has used this phrase as a means of suppressing news it considers compromising. A Congressional subcommittee on government information found that various government agencies stamped a security label on numerous reports which had nothing to do with security. It found, for example, that the Pentagon attempted to hide a list of generals who got flight pay without flying. It also was discovered that the Army delayed the announcement of helicopter tests to gain wider publicity, even though no security was involved.

In his book, *The Pentagon Propaganda Machine,* U.S. Senator J. W. Fulbright recounts how Admiral Thomas H. Moorer, former Chief of Naval Operations, told a veterans' group that the nation had not lost an aircraft carrier "in some fifty wars or near-wars since 1946." When Minnesota Senator Walter F. Mondale asked the admiral for a list of the conflicts, Moorer supplied forty-eight examples, but requested that they be kept classified. Mondale insisted the information should be made public and the admiral declassified all but a few. Except for the wars in Korea and Vietnam, the list contained mostly "alerts" in different parts of the world, only a few of which involved the United States.

"To be charitable to the Navy," Senator Mondale observed, "I would say the most embarrassing incidents remained classified."

Secrecy prevails in every branch of the government, despite the passage a few years ago of a Freedom of Information Act, the purpose of which was to make non-security files and records available to the public. In 1972 a Congressional committee headed by Representative William S. Moorhead, of Pennsylvania, concluded that the act had been hampered by "five years of foot-dragging by the federal bureaucracy." Despite such hindrance, the new law has opened up more information by giving the news media a means to sue for release if an official insists on keeping the lid on a particular piece of information. The Nashville *Tennessean* and the Philadelphia *Inquirer* have won court cases for exposure of federal records.

In June, 1972, President Nixon ordered the complete revamping of the system for classifying and controlling national security information. The new rule, which was welcomed by the press and others, drastically cut the number of government agencies authorized to use secrecy stamps and required each official with stamping power to be so designated by his boss in writing. In the first two months of the order, the number of bureaucrats entitled to handle the stamps dropped by 63 percent. Nevertheless, about sixteen thousand government employees still have the power to paste classification marks on documents.

Two years ago, the Senate Subcommittee on Security Agreements and Commitments Abroad reported that the executive branch consistently overclassified information relating to foreign policy that should be a matter of public record. Senator Stuart Symington, committee chairman, called the tendency to overclassify a part of the process of "creeping commitments." This, he explained, is a policy which forces the U.S.

government to practice deception as a means of protecting secret agreements with other countries. The subcommittee gave the following examples of "creeping commitments." The government of Thailand did not want it known that the U.S. was using air bases in that country. Laos did not want it revealed that this country was fighting a major war action there. The Philippine government wanted to conceal the fact that the U.S. was paying sizable allowances to the Philippine non-combat force that went to Vietnam.

Reporters during the Nixon administration found their way blocked to other executive departments as well as to the President himself. In the summer of 1973, the State Department Correspondents Association sent a resolution to then Secretary of State William Rogers protesting the "deterioration in the flow of information." The newsmen said they were concerned "about the infrequent meetings with the secretary and other senior officials." They noted that Rogers had not held a press conference in Washington for six months.

The United States Congress can play the secrecy game as well as can the executive department on occasion. For every open Watergate hearing, there are dozens of closed meetings of Congressional committees. A 1971 survey by the *Congressional Quarterly* showed that of the House committees that held more than one hundred meetings each, the number of secret sessions jumped 41 percent over the previous year. The Appropriations Committee closed all of its meetings; Agriculture, 75 percent; Ways and Means, 70 percent; and Armed Services, 57 percent. Only two Senate committees—Armed Services and Foreign Relations—held less than 50 percent of their meetings in private. In 1972, more than one-third of all U.S. Senate committee sessions were closed. Senate and House committees and subcommittees operated behind closed doors 40 percent of the time, according to the *Congressional Quarterly*. The executive or "mark-up" sessions (where real action or decision takes place) were held in secrecy 79 percent of the time in the House and 98 percent of the time in the Senate. All these meetings involved the public's interest.

Secrecy persisted in Congress despite the 1970 Reorganization Act, which was designed to bring more meetings out into the open. The media feel that Congressional withholding of information is just as odious as that done by the President or anyone else at the executive level. The *Washington Post* commented in an editorial: "Maximum openness ought to be the aim of Congress. Nothing serves better to promote public confidence in the integrity of a legislative body; nothing does more to foster public understanding of legislative processes and problems. It is after all the public's business which Congress and its committees are discussing."

Congressman F. Edward Hébert, of Louisiana, defended closed committee hearings. He said he believed in having open meetings as often as possible but declared that the issue had been "exaggerated by the news media." "The only disadvantage to a closed meeting is lack of understanding on the part of the public," he added.

Former U.S. Senator Albert Gore, of Tennessee, told a civil liberties panel in 1973:

I would not lightly overlook the secrecy involved in security and in international affairs. True, every administration I have known—Roosevelt to Nixon—would readily hide behind this often phony shield, but there have been and will be real reasons for secrecy in both diplomacy and in military intelligence.

There are other instances where secrecy in the legislative process is advisable—examination of individual tax returns in the course of study for tax legislation, for example.

But to acknowledge the justification for secrecy in some instances but serves to prove the virtue generally of public procedure. As I retrospectively contemplate the many secret sessions of the U.S. Senate Foreign Relations Committee, on which I served during the tragic years of the Vietnam war, I now believe the nation would have been better served if all these sessions had been public. . . .

Sinister motives are not always involved when elected officials want to meet behind closed doors. Without the press and public present, the members feel free to let down their hair. They can make unflattering remarks about absent individuals and can engage in heated arguments with each other without worrying about being overheard. Some congressmen also are not anxious to have others know precisely how they arrived at a particular decision.

State and Local Government Access

The press's lack of access to news sources is not only a Washington problem. Secrecy in state and local government is widespread. It has a direct effect on the public as well as on the news media. Ordinary citizens are not normally privileged to attend Presidential news conferences, interview cabinet officers, or sit in on Senate committee meetings. But they do expect admittance to meetings of school boards, city councils, boards of supervisors, and zoning commissions. In a number of communities, the public and the press are not invited to these gatherings. Nor do they get news from any other sources. Secret meetings, hidden records, and uncommunicative officials are commonplace in both the statehouse and city hall.

As of this writing, thirty-three states have both open-meeting and open-record laws. Under these regulations, public officials must conduct open meetings and make public records available to the press and public. Most of the meeting laws contain exceptions for "executive sessions" in which sensitive personnel matters are discussed. Although closed meetings and concealed files are more prevalent in states lacking such statutes, clandestine government prevails to one degree or another in all fifty states. In some areas, local bodies go to amazing lengths to keep out of public sight. They meet in private homes, members' offices, firehouses, restaurants, and over barbecue roasts. Their favorite ploy is to debate the pros and cons of an issue in secret and then rubber-stamp their actions at a public meeting. In this way, the press or public has little or no inkling of the factors or arguments that prompt decisions. The legislature of Orange County, New York, drew up its 1973 budget in secret because, as one member put it, "We get more work done that way." In Kansas City, Missouri, the mayor suggested last year that the city council go into closed session to debate two matters of vital concern to the public: the use of promised federal revenue-sharing money and the planning of a capital-improvements program.

The Des Moines, Iowa, City Council held a private meeting in the mayor's office in apparent violation of state law. His Honor denied there had been a meeting at all, terming it rather "an informal discussion." A newspaperman and Sigma Delta Chi, the journalistic society, sued the Charlotte, North Carolina, City Council for holding a secret session to consider a downtown parking garage. And in Flint, Michigan, the city council lost a court suit over its contention that it had a right to meet behind locked doors in preparation for its regular open meeting. The legal action was taken by the local newspaper, which espoused the position that councilmen should be required to discuss public business in public view. In Meriden, Connecticut, the town newspaper revealed that the school board had raised the school superintendent's salary and created new school titles but did not announce the resolutions until seven weeks later.

Local and state officials are also adept at keeping public records from prying reporters. Newsmen in some localities are blocked from inspecting police logs, building permits, welfare rolls, and other files. Sometimes, the news media can gain access to public documents only with a court order. The Monmouth (N.J.) *Courier* won a legal fight in 1971 to force Middletown

Township officials to bring out the records of a sub-division purchase. In Williamson, West Virginia, the *Daily News* went to court to force the mayor and police chief to let reporters look at arrest records.

Newsmen find it hard to carry out their normal duties when records are inaccessible. A police reporter who cannot look at the police blotter is of little value to his newspaper or broadcast station. A county court reporter or a statehouse correspondent checks records and statistics as part of his job.

Why can't the reporters get to the records? The reasons vary. Some officials embrace secrecy for its own sake. They can't adjust to the idea that they are serving the public which pays them. Other motives are more obvious. The police chief is feuding with the local newspaper and decides to make things as difficult as possible for its reporters. A city council which has awarded sewer bids to the brother of one of its members, even though he was the high bidder, isn't anxious to let the news out. Minor clerks and other low-ranking employees are often not sure of what they can and cannot release, so they play it safe by releasing nothing. Hidden records also can mask embezzlement and other crimes. Scores of public officials, including former governors, U.S. senators, and mayors have been sentenced to prison terms on the basis of records and files that proved their misdeeds.

Shutting off the news by gag rule is another cause of friction between the press and local government. The mayors of Honolulu and Milwaukee have denied reporters admittance to their offices. Mayor Frank Rizzo of Philadelphia threatened to cut off the *Bulletin* from official news after the newspaper reported a "political espionage" police unit. In a boiling telephone conversation with *Bulletin* city editor John J. Farmer, Rizzo reportedly said: "John, don't bother to call me or any of my people in city government anymore. There'll be no response. I won't respond to this unfair treatment. . . . Not a thing will appear in your paper about city government."

Last year, the mayor of Cheyenne, Wyoming, ordered city departments to clear all news releases with
him before distributing them to the press. Other mayors
and city managers have employed the same tactic to
control the news. The Hartsville, South Carolina, City
Council adopted a resolution that it must OK any town
news before it is released to the media.

All these actions by administrative and legislative
sources have strained press relations at the state and
local levels. Although the public has a clear stake in
the problem, it has given the media little support. Indeed, it is not uncommon for citizens to side with the
city council or mayor in their battles with the press.

"The press is viewed as the antagonist in its fights
with politicians," said David Laventhol, editor of
Newsday. "The politicians know this and play us off
against the public whose support they count on. The
public has little understanding of the First Amendment. If we take on a local government agency about
secrecy or other wrongdoing, we are often accused
by people of interfering with correct process. When one
of our investigative stories concerning politicians is
published we are often attacked by readers. 'Why are
you doing this?' they say."

Mr. Laventhol's remarks would indicate that the
press still has a credibility problem with the public.
Many people stand behind public officials on the access
issue, despite evidence that they are being denied their
democratic right to know what's going on in their federal, state, or local government. The antipress sentiment
disseminated by the Nixon administration and by public
officials throughout the country has apparently convinced numbers of people that somehow the press is
wrong and that government secrecy is right.

It seems advisable for the media to woo the public
to their camp by means of a public relations campaign.
Newspapers, magazines, and broadcast stations should
spend more time and effort explaining to their audiences what they have to gain by supporting the press
in the right-to-know conflict. At the same time, news-

men and women should strive harder for accuracy
and fairness in presenting the news. The loss of credibility is not wholly the fault of hostile public officials.
When the media err frequently and are unbalanced in
their reporting, the public cannot be expected to place
blind faith in them. Newspapers and broadcasters must
remember that, like the officeholder, they, too, carry a
public trust. Today, the need is greater than ever for
balanced reporting that serves not the politicians or
any special interest, but the public at large.

CHAPTER SEVEN

The Media and the Law

AMERICAN JOURNALISTS HAD gone to jail in the past but on June 29, 1972, the U.S. Supreme Court made the practice the law of the land under certain circumstances. The high court, in a landmark decision, ruled five to four that the First Amendment does not grant reporters immunity from disclosing material received from confidential sources. The decision meant that newsmen can be put behind bars for refusing to tell where they got their information. The ruling was delivered in the combined cases of three newsmen: Earl Caldwell of *The New York Times,* Paul M. Branzburg of the *Louisville Courier-Journal,* and Paul Pappas, a reporter-cameraman for WTEV-TV in New Bedford, Massachusetts.

The judgment aroused newsmen throughout the nation and led to their support for a federal "shield" law to protect reporters in future confrontations with law enforcement officials on the issue of immunity. The Department of Justice took the position that reporters have a duty to reveal information about an actual or potential crime just as does any other citizen. Further, the government contended, newsmen can lawfully be subpoenaed to testify before a grand jury. The press has traditionally held that disclosure to grand juries or law enforcement officials of confidential sources of information would dry up these sources and thereby dam the flow of news to the public. Journalists argue that certain informants will talk to them only if they are promised anonymity. Such sources could include politicians, left-wing or right-wing militants, criminals, city officials, lawyers, businessmen, and even police officers. Reporters say that if they break their pledge of silence, their sources will no longer trust them with information. Thus, the newsmen reason, without sources they are of no use to their newspapers or broadcast stations and the public is the final loser.

The cases of the three reporters in the Supreme Court ruling clearly illustrate the issue.

Caldwell, a black reporter in the *Times*'s San Francisco bureau, was called before a grand jury after he had written a series of articles on the Black Panthers. In one of the stories, he quoted a Panther leader as

UPI

UPI's Supreme Court reporter Charlotte Moulton at work in the UPI booth below court chambers. She has covered the Supreme Court for UPI since 1949 and is a recognized expert in reporting and interpreting its decisions.

having said that blacks must engage in an "armed struggle" to obtain their civil rights. The Justice Department subpoenaed him to tell the grand jury the source of the remark and about a reputed Panther arms cache. Caldwell replied that if he were compelled to appear and testify his effectiveness as a reporter would be destroyed because the Black Panthers would know he had violated their confidence and would lose faith in him.

The Federal District Court refused to quash the subpoena and ordered him to appear before the grand jury. The court said he would not be required to disclose confidential sources of information or to answer questions about matters not given him for publication. Caldwell still declined to appear and the court found him guilty of contempt and sentenced him to jail. The sentence was suspended pending the outcome of appeals. The U.S. Ninth Circuit Court of Appeals in San Francisco reversed the lower court on the grounds that its order did not properly protect Caldwell's First Amendment rights. The appeals court said the reporter did not have to appear before the grand jury unless the Department of Justice could prove a "compelling need" for his testimony. When the case went up to the Supreme Court it was on the question of whether a newsman has an *absolute* right to refuse to appear before a grand jury unless the government can show a compelling need for his information.

In explaining his position some months later before the American Newspaper Publishers Association, Caldwell said that he found that even as a black man, the job of covering the Black Panthers was not easy.

"Right away they pinned the cop label on me," the reporter recounted. "Finally, after telling them every day that I was a reporter, not a police agent, they let me get close enough to write stories deeper than those you get at press conferences. I was able after a while to get into their office whenever I wanted. . . . I got the opportunity to observe their breakfast program firsthand. . . . I was able to get into a position to write about who and what they were, and it took me a long time to convince them that my only interest in them was to get information for *The New York Times*. I was not always pleased where the paper displayed the stories, but they were always published."

Branzburg ran into the same kind of problem while digging out a story on drugs. He was subpoenaed by two county grand juries after he had written two articles on the subject. One related how two unidentified young men were experimenting for a way to make salable hashish from marijuana. The other discussed the scope of marijuana and other drug usage in the Louisville area.

Like Caldwell, Branzburg refused to appear before the grand jury. He cited a Kentucky shield law that grants newsmen immunity from disclosing confidential sources.

Pappas' legal troubles also arose from his coverage of the Black Panthers. He had taken part in reporting racial disturbances in the New Bedford area and had been invited by the Panthers to visit their headquarters at the time a police raid was expected. He was informed by the black group that he could take pictures of the raid but could not report anything else that went on inside the building. The raid did not come off and Pappas reported nothing. The grand jury wanted to hear his story anyway and subpoenaed him. He refused to appear, despite an order by the Massachusetts Supreme Court that he had to.

According to Caldwell, government subpoena power limits the ability of any reporter—black or white—to operate effectively. "If I was going to continue as a reporter with credibility at all, I could not comply with the court order," he explained.

Caldwell and other reporters have said they have been forced to destroy tapes and other records of interviews for fear they will be subpoenaed and disclosed.

The Supreme Court ruling against the three newsmen touched off one of the most significant debates in the history of American journalism. It provoked a wave of subpoenas and contempt-of-court citations against newsmen and ignited an intense discussion of how far the government can go before it interferes with the public's right to a free flow of information.

The first newsman to land in jail under the high court's order was Peter J. Bridge, a hard-nosed veteran reporter for the now defunct *Newark News*. He was found guilty of contempt of court for failing to answer five questions before a grand jury in connection with his story about a purported bribe attempt of a Newark city official. The 36-year-old newsman contended that his effectiveness as a reporter would be eroded if he went beyond the facts in his published article. For his refusal to testify, Bridge spent twenty days in jail during which time he became a symbol for those who sought a federal law protecting a journalist's right to confidentiality.

Following his release, Bridge said he chose jail "on principle." "The basic issue," he continued, "is not a press issue but a people issue. Newsmen were invested with responsibility to inform the public and must be protected in the exercise of that responsibility."

Also standing on principle was William T. Farr, a *Los Angeles Times* reporter who spent forty-seven days in jail for not revealing to a judge sources of information he had received in confidence. Farr, who was then a newsman for the *Los Angeles Herald-Examiner,* had published a story dealing with the Charles Manson murder trial in 1970. The article was based on a pre-trial transcript of testimony that Manson was plotting the murder of several Hollywood celebrities. One of the eight lawyers in the trial had released the testimony to Farr and Superior Court Judge Charles H. Holder demanded to know which one. When Farr, in the privacy of the judge's chambers, refused to name the source, Holder called him "a martyr without a cause" and placed him behind bars on thirteen counts of civil contempt. The reporter was isolated in a cell of his own and was not allowed to have a typewriter or any books unless they came from the public library. He was not permitted to mingle with other prisoners.

Another newsman, John F. Lawrence, Washington bureau chief for the *Los Angeles Times*, was jailed for a few hours in December of 1972, when he refused to surrender tape recordings of an interview with a principal witness in the bugging of Democratic party headquarters at the Watergate apartments. Three days later, the newspaper turned over the tapes to a federal judge after the witness released the paper from its pledge of confidentiality. Jack Nelson, one of the reporters who taped the interview, said the resolution was proper under the circumstances but noted that the larger question remained: whether a reporter can be forced to give up confidential notes or tapes. The Reporters Committee for Freedom of the Press, an organization of Washington journalists, was unhappy with the outcome and issued this statement: "We think this case represents a further serious erosion of freedom of the press. After all, two federal courts did order the *Los Angeles Times* bureau chief to jail. The only reason he escaped further imprisonment was not the protection of the First Amendment but because a news source backed down on the confidentiality privilege."

David M. Lightman, a Baltimore *Evening Sun* reporter, answered the questions of a Worcester County, Maryland, grand jury on June 12, 1973, rather than go to jail. The case went back to 1971, when Lightman was first called before the grand jury and refused to describe an Ocean City pipe shop owner who offered him marijuana while a policeman was in the shop. The presiding judge cited the reporter for contempt. Lightman appealed all the way to the U.S. Supreme Court and lost. When the grand jury called him again, he gave the information.

Joseph Weiler, a Memphis *Commercial-Appeal* reporter, also got into trouble with the law over confidentiality. In 1972, he was ordered to appear before a Tennessee State Senate investigating committee and divulge his sources for a story on child abuse at a state hospital for retarded youngsters. The newspaper had received an anonymous tip about child beatings at the institution and Weiler was assigned to track it down.

Angus McEachran, the *Commercial-Appeal*'s assistant managing editor, gave this account of the incident, according to an article by Carol Ternovesky in the December, 1972, issue of *Quill* Magazine: "Weiler said he thought it would be a good story but that people's jobs were at stake, and he would not be able to divulge any names. He had been given the names of persons fired for child abuse, and he also checked with those presently employed.

"Curiously, the state senators zeroed in, not on the child beaters, but on the reporter, who dared to bring the condition to public light. They hauled Joe Weiler in front of them and told him to bring his notes and correspondence with him. The entire investigation seemed to be concentrated on their effort to find out which state employee had tipped off the newspapers to what was happening at the hospital."

When Weiler balked at revealing his sources, he was asked to show cause why he should not be held in contempt. The case was on appeal at this writing.

McEachran said the Weiler case convinced him of the need for a federal or state shield law protecting reporters in similar situations. However, he warned that "whenever you start to define the rights of the press, you run the great risk of limiting these rights. I see a great danger in the misconception of such a bill. I think we ought to stop referring to it as a 'Shield Law' or 'Newsmen's Privilege Law.' We really aren't talking about the newsman's privilege, but the people's right to know."

By way of making his point, the editor observed: "Should child abuse become a problem at Arlington again, it would take a small miracle for someone to pick up the phone and call the *Commercial-Appeal*."

The broadcast industry also felt the government's

subpoena power. Among the victims was Edwin Goodman, manager of WBAI-FM, a listener-sponsored radio station in New York City.

Goodman was sentenced to a thirty-day contempt of court sentence for refusing to turn over to the district attorney tapes of telephone conversations recorded during a prison riot. The DA subpoenaed thirty hours of taped recordings and also demanded the station's pertinent program logs. Goodman surrendered the logs but refused to give up the tapes, citing New York's "newsmen's privilege" law, which was designed to protect newsmen from contempt for failing to disclose news or the source of news. The station manager defied a State Supreme Court order to hand over the tapes. He spent forty-four hours in jail before he was released pending appeal of the sentence.

In recapping the case for the May, 1972, issue of *WBAI,* the station's magazine, Goodman's lawyers noted:

At the Friday hearing in the Supreme Court, Justice [Gerald] Culkin invoked a power, reserved by law for those rare occasions of imminent and actual disruption of judicial proceedings, to hold WBAI and Ed Goodman summarily in contempt. No hearing was had, no witnesses were permitted to testify, not even the minimal showing of need for the materials subpoenaed was required from the DA and Ed Goodman was denied the most fundamental right to address the court. Rather, the station was held in contempt and fined $250 and Ed Goodman sentenced to 30 days in the civil jail. Motions to stay execution of the sentence or release him on bail were rejected. The last refusal appears to be unprecedented; reporters and other newspeople have gone to jail in the past, but not until their legal claims were finally determined and rejected on appeal.

In the cases of newsmen involved in privilege conflicts with the courts, confidential sources are seldom used for direct quotes. More often, they provide tips, leads, and insights that can be confirmed elsewhere. The first phone call is merely the start of what can be a long process before a story is ever published.

Vincent A. Blasi, University of Michigan law professor, made a 1971 study based on interviews with hundreds of reporters on their dealings with confidential sources. He concluded: "The reporters most hindered by the possibility of being subpoenaed are those who seek a composite picture, who check and cross-check their information with numerous sources."

However, Blasi also found that most of the journalists interviewed believed that the profession relies too much on "off-the-record information and not-for-attribution quotes."

"They offer several reasons for thinking that the reliance on this type of information is, in many ways, a bad journalistic habit," he said. "For one thing, reporters can get caught up in a gossip syndrome. They could become more concerned with getting the inside story *for themselves* than with getting as much information as possible to the reader. Many newsmen feel that reporters can get a great deal more information on-the-record if they were tougher with sources and less concerned about being on the inside. . . . Another danger with confidential sources is that the sources tend to lie more readily when the discussion is off-the-record, knowing their deceit will not be exposed."

Nevertheless, more than 90 percent of the newsmen in the survey told Blasi they would go to jail rather than reveal their sources.

"If press subpoenas will produce more martyrs than evidence, what is the point?" Blasi asked.

Those seeking reporters' testimony apparently worried little whether the newsmen would become martyrs or not. At the height of the shield controversy in 1973, the Committee to Re-elect President Nixon issued a dozen subpoenas in connection with the bugging of the Democratic National Committee Headquarters. Named in the orders were reporters and executives of *The New York Times,* the *Washington Post,* the *Washington Star-News,* and *Time* Magazine. The committee was embroiled in a series of lawsuits and countersuits over the bugging and sought the newsmen's notes, tapes, films, and other private material that would abet its case. In fighting the action, *Times* publisher Arthur Ochs Sulzberger stated that the subpoena on the paper's reporter, John Crewdson, "violates the basic First Amendment rights of the *Times,* its reporters and the public."

Others subpoenaed included Katherine Graham, publisher of the *Washington Post,* and Howard Simons, the paper's managing editor.

Many media people believe that the only way the confidentiality question will be resolved is by enactment of a federal shield law to prevent reporters from being forced to disclose sources. Both the House and the Senate are currently studying such a measure. Nineteen states currently have such laws, including California and New Jersey, where Farr and Bridge respectively were jailed. The state statutes range from those providing complete immunity to others containing loopholes to allow for disclosure under certain circumstances.

The issue of a national shield law is complicated by the fact that newsmen themselves are not in agreement on just what kind of a bill it should be. A random sampling by Associated Press bureaus of reporters on investigative assignments showed an almost fifty-fifty split between advocates of absolute confidentiality and those favoring only limited protection of news sources.

"I don't want a shield law. None. I'll take my chances with the Constitution," said Ed Pound, of the *Chicago Sun-Times.*

"A shield law would be another government participation in my trade," commented Jeff Nesmith, of *The Atlanta Constitution,* a winner of the Georgia Associated Press award for investigative reporting into organized crime.

The opposite reaction came from Bill Lynch, of the New Orleans *States-Item,* who felt that "only an unqualified shield law can adequately protect newsmen from overzealous and retaliatory public officials ill-disposed to the exposure of the truth." Warren Hoge, of the *New York Post,* and Richard Oliver, of the *New York Daily News,* both opted for absolute shield laws.

Editors, too, are divided on the wording of shield laws. At a 1973 convention of the American Society of Newspaper Editors a show of hands was asked in answer to three questions: Who favored an absolute bill? Who favored a qualified bill? Who preferred no bill at all? About 25 percent of the five hundred editors called for an absolute shield law and about an equal number leaned toward a qualified bill. *But most indicated they would be happiest with no bill at all.*

John Lawrence, the *Los Angeles Times* Washington bureau chief, who went to jail on the issue, was among the editors favoring an airtight bill. His position was challenged by Charles Bennett, of the Oklahoma *Times,* who reminded the audience that investigative reporters had uncovered the Watergate scandal without shield legislation.

U.S. Senator Alan Cranston of California, who is co-author with Senator Edward Kennedy of Massachusetts of the strongest protective bill introduced in Congress, told the editors that Watergate demonstrated the need for an absolute bill. He urged the media to press for enactment of his proposal.

Proponents of an absolute shield were taken aback when Clark Mollenhoff, one of the best investigative reporters in the nation, told a Congressional committee that "an absolute shield law would represent a dilution of the First Amendment."

Mollenhoff, a Pulitzer Prize winner, who is chief of the Des Moines *Register*'s Washington bureau, said an absolute statute would do four things:

1. "It would cover every potential pamphleteer as part of the press entitled to have his confidential sources protected."

2. "This would mean that every person who had written a book, an article or a pamphlet, or anyone who could claim he was gathering information for a book, article or pamphlet."

3. "It would cover all confidential information on all crimes from petty larceny to murder obtained while news-gathering."

4. "It would cover all investigative forms from county grand juries to Congressional hearings, and would certainly include regulatory agencies established to protect the public interest on everything from air safety to environmental protection."

A shield bill, according to Mollenhoff, would "create total chaos in those government bodies that must use the subpoena power to obtain witnesses and documents in an effort to elicit the truth. It would be a disaster to organized government, business, and labor."

Mollenhoff noted that, as an investigator for thirty years, he had always protected his sources before grand juries, citing the First Amendment as the only weapon he needed. "An absolute shield law would hurt the press because it would promote irresponsibility and lack of accountability," he declared.

The pro-shield forces suffered another severe setback when former New Jersey Governor William T. Cahill vetoed in 1972 what was hailed as the strongest news source protection legislation in the country. In defending his action, Cahill said: "While freedom of the press is one of our most important Constitutional principles, there are other very well-accepted rights of our citizens which clearly come into conflict with this principle. In our American system of government, checks and balances have always played a major role in the control of limited power. It is no more acceptable to have the press all powerful than it is to have government all powerful."

The New Jersey chapter of the American Civil Liberties Union called the veto a "cruel blow to a free press."

Four months later, Governor Cahill again upheld his veto—this time at the New Jersey Press Association's annual convention in Atlantic City. He asserted that his action was a safeguard against "irresponsible news people." He referred specifically to the admission of a "goof" by syndicated columnist Jack Anderson in his reporting that Senator Thomas F. Eagleton, George McGovern's running mate in the 1972 presidential campaign, had been guilty of drunken driving. Eagleton denied the charge and Anderson later apologized, admitting he had erred.

"Which of the two would you have believed?" Cahill asked the publishers. "The candidate for high office or the columnist who is circulated in hundreds of newspapers?"

The New Jersey bill actually was a tightening of an existing shield law which had not been strong enough to save Peter Bridge from jail.

But media supporters of shield legislation got a welcome boost from a highly prestigious source, the Association of the Bar of the City of New York. The group submitted to the House Judiciary Committee a recommendation for a protective bill that read in part:

After reviewing the constitutional and policy issues posed by these legislative proposals, we have concluded that creation of journalists' privilege by Federal legislation is authorized by the Constitution and that enactment of legislation to disclose confidential source relationships would advance the fundamental values inherent in the freedom of the press under the First Amendment without unduly hampering the legitimate interests of law enforcement.

We believe the qualified privilege to be created by such Federal legislation should be applicable against State as well as Federal investigatory bodies, that it should be invoked only by professional journalists and that the privilege should defer to certain carefully defined investigative needs of special urgency. . . .

The public supports a shield law, according to a 1972 survey by the American Institute of Public Opinion. The study indicated that most people in the United States are on the side of reporters who refuse to identify their sources in official inquiries. Based on interviews with 1,462 adults 18 and older in more than 300 localities across the country, the researchers found that 57 percent held the view that a newspaper reporter "should not be required to reveal confidential sources if taken to court to testify about information appearing in a news article." Thirty-four percent thought the reporter should identify his source. College-educated persons made up the bulk of the respondents favoring reporters' confidentiality rights.

It seems evident that newsmen's privilege is an issue of growing importance and involves more than just a conflict between the media and the courts. The public has a big stake in the question since the flow of information could be affected. And, of course, the process of justice is also a matter that concerns Americans.

There are, however, some aspects of the situation which, perhaps, need clarification. First, it should be understood that it is the investigative reporter who would be most affected by shield legislation or lack of it. This journalist is not normally occupied with daily spot news stories. He may spend several weeks chasing down leads, which come from various sources. The true investigative newsman is not put off easily by roadblocks. There is a strong possibility that, if faced with the fact of no confidentiality privileges, he would find some other way to obtain the information if a source demanded anonymity. Journalistic enterprise will somehow prevail as it always has. It should be kept in mind, too, that some sources have their own reasons for disclosing information and would do so even if it meant they risked exposure. For example, a policeman who has been dismissed from the force may be anxious to settle a score with those he believes responsible. Therefore, if his story involves police corruption, he is perhaps less interested in cleaning up the department than in getting his revenge. For this, he may be willing to take a chance on having his name come out.

Second, some district attorneys, although dedicated to the cause of justice, are equally anxious to have newsmen act as their investigators in criminal cases. Peter Bridge, the New Jersey reporter jailed for sheltering his source, has claimed that the prosecutor "wanted me to do his work." When this occurs, an ethical situation arises for the reporter. He is not a law officer. His basic responsibility is to report the news, not arrest criminals. If he sees a crime committed on the street, he, like any other citizen, has an obligation to notify police, but he is not on full-time duty as a detective.

Finally, we must ask if the First Amendment does offer sufficient legal backing for reporters up against grand juries in confidentiality cases. The Constitution guarantees freedom of the press but does not spell out the press's responsibilities. Interpretation of the amendment is often a matter of who is making the interpretation. A liberal-minded judge may hold (and has done so) that newsmen can stand squarely behind the First Amendment when it comes to testifying about sources. Another jurist may see the issue differently in light of the Constitution.

The political climate also is an element to be considered. It is not mere coincidence that a wave of reporter jailings came at a time when the media were under intensive attack by the administration and other segments of our society. Whereas the First Amendment might have proved adequate during some other period, it has failed in many instances to keep newsmen from being cited for contempt. When the Watergate scandal was laid bare and the press was credited with a major role in the disclosure, there occurred a significant dropping-off in the number of reporters being locked up for protecting their sources. It is precisely for this reason that many newsmen do not want to leave interpretation of the First Amendment to the whims of fate and the political atmosphere. They feel that once a tough law is passed, the temper of judges or of the times will not hamstring them in undertaking investigative reporting.

The tide appears to be running in favor of some kind of federal privilege legislation for newsmen. Whether it will be a strong or weak law remains to be seen. At the moment, there is widespread doubt that Congress will enact an absolutely unqualified shield bill. The dilemma presented by the controversy was summed up by North Carolina Senator Sam J. Ervin, Jr., Chairman of the Judiciary Subcommittee. After listening to a parade of witnesses on both sides of the issue, he commented: "I could make a good argument for either one."

CHAPTER EIGHT

A Matter of Ethics

THERE ARE TIMES when the news media act as the nation's conscience. Editorials condemn the venality of politicians and corruption in office. If there is a slippage in public morals or a slackness in national purpose, some newspaper, magazine, or broadcast station is sure to deplore the trend. The media give us advice on protecting the environment, driving the highways, preventing forest fires, and voting. If there is a political or social controversy, a large sector of the media has an opinion one way or the other.

Few would doubt that part of the media's responsibility is to guide the public in matters on which they may have more information. At the same time, however, it is only fair to ask about the morals and character of those seeking to instruct us. In short, how ethical and honest are the media?

The answer is complex. News people themselves disagree on what constitutes unethical behavior. Rules of conduct differ on various newspapers, magazines, and broadcast outlets. Some ethical violations are, of course, so blatant that they are universally disapproved in the media. In the case of others, the shadings are not so clearly drawn. The question of gifts and favors to newsmen is a prime example.

There is hardly a reporter alive who, at one time or another, has not eaten a meal supplied by a news source. Many news events are tied into lunches or dinners at hotels, restaurants, and other places. Frequently, the host provides a press table around which reporters take notes on a speech or announcement. Seldom do the media representatives pay the check, which may also include preliminary cocktails and wine.

This practice is standard and only a naive newsmaker would assume that reporters can be bought with a free lunch or dinner. The newsman himself gives little thought to the matter. He is assigned to cover the story whether it takes place at the Waldorf Astoria Hotel or at the Salvation Army soup kitchen. Further, he can't cover the event from outside the building. And since it's lunch time, he has to eat somewhere. The most thorough study would be unlikely to unearth any significant correlation between favorable news stories and courtesy lunches and dinners for reporters.

Unfortunately, the "freebie" practice doesn't stop with meals. There was, for instance, the columnist for a Detroit newspaper who was found to have seven cars listed in his name—all given him by automobile manufacturers. A *New York* Magazine article revealed that New York daily newspapers receive thousands of dollars worth of free tickets to sports events at Madison Square Garden. Newspaper and magazine travel writers are regularly flown to exotic places, with all expenses paid by airline companies and hotels. Fashion editors and food writers receive a large amount of booty from manufacturers. *The National Observer* reported in a 1971 article that media men and women assigned to the Men's Fashion Association "press week" were the recipients of lavish gifts and wide-open hospitality. The loot included cosmetics, gold necklaces, clothing, fourteen banquet-sized meals, and "enough liquor to float a barge." One entertainer alone—Sears Roebuck and Co.—picked up a tab of forty-seven thousand dollars.

Other newsmen and women around the country have accepted color television sets, cases of liquor, golf clubs and other prizes. *Quill* Magazine told of a marketing writer who wrote a complimentary story about the diaper industry at a time when his wife was pregnant. He was supplied with more than enough sample diapers and baby products. A Detroit auto manufacturer invited the press to attend the unveiling of a new model car and thoughtfully laid an expensive camera at the plate of each reporter or editor attending the luncheon. Nevada gambling casinos are extremely generous in distributing gifts to friendly newsmen.

The list continues. Free theater tickets are commonly handed out to critics. Some sports writers travel and are housed at the expense of local baseball or football teams. Complimentary passes to racetracks, movies, circuses, baseball games, etc., regularly find their way into editors' desks for distribution to staff members. Largesse also is heaped on newsmen in the form of self-serving "journalism awards" sponsored by the Thoroughbred Racing Association, the American Bowling Congress, the National Association of Engine and Boat Manufacturers, the National Association of Real Estate Boards, and other such organizations. The Cigar Institute of America offers press photographers cash awards for news pictures of people smoking cigars —if the pictures are published.

The public has every right to be suspicious of news organizations and news personnel who are "on the take." Some gifts, such as complimentary lunches at news events and an occasional bottle of liquor at Christmas, are harmless. Others, however, reflect seriously on the press's credibility and its role as a guide and informer. *Quill* hit the issue squarely when it said (August, 1973): "A growing consciousness of public disillusionment with the press requires some sort of re-evaluation, so one obvious avenue is to put into practice, either institutionally or personally, professional standards of ethics."

In his book, *Pressures on the Press,* Professor Hillier Kreighbaum saw the danger this way: "Possible conflicts of interest are a constant threat to newsroom objectivity and one does not have to be playing for

big financial payoffs. . . . Responsible journalists are
well aware of the hazards. Offerings come in all sizes,
from a free drink at some lobbyist's party to outright
acceptance of cash or checks. Others might include an
offer for a free trip to a war zone in an Air Force jet
with room and food in officers' quarters during the
stay, an all-expenses-paid tour by an auto manufacturer to see new models, an invitation from an overseas hotel corporation to visit a new installation, or a
visit to a local professional baseball team at spring
training camp. The objective each time is to generate
favorable coverage that otherwise would not take
place."

There is no question that expensive gifts and favors
dispensed to a newsman by news sources are a not
too subtle form of bribery. It doesn't always work;
it may not work most of the time. But the im-
plication is there. The reporter who accepts the gra-
tuity is compromised, whether or not he responds by
writing a flattering story. The old adage that nothing is
ever free holds in this kind of situation. If the press is
to command public respect, the people who write and
broadcast for it must be above suspicion. How can
readers or viewers believe anything the media tell
them if they know that reporters, editors, announcers,
and management executives are getting payola?

Media managers have taken a hard look at gifts and
favors in recent years and, in numerous instances, have
stopped the practice. Stringent codes of ethics have
been imposed on staffers, who have been warned they
face the loss of their jobs for violating the rules. The
day after *New York* Magazine published the article
about the free tickets to Madison Square Garden, *The
New York Times* posted this memo: "We are of this
day putting into effect a new policy with regard to
complimentary tickets to sports events. From now on
we will accept none. . . ." The note added that all
tickets on hand would be returned or canceled and that
managements of sports promotions would be informed
of the new policy by the sports editor. Managing

editor A. M. Rosenthal notified staffers that if they felt a professional need to attend a sports event, the sports editor would purchase a ticket for them.

A 1973 survey by *Quill* of newspaper managing editors and radio and TV news directors turned up some strict policies against freebies and some that were less strict. The Camden (N.J.) *Courier-Post,* the *Detroit Free Press,* and the *Hartford* (Conn.) *Courant* claimed they completely forbade acceptance of tickets, dinners, junkets, and gifts from public sources. William J. Clew, of the *Courant,* said further, "Our sports department staff cannot serve as officials of any sports contest, or as officers of any sports organization, or take part in any sports activity that might reflect on our integrity. We probably have the strictest rules of conduct of any sports staff in the country."

The *Denver Post* said it had tough rules against solicitation of any kind and would permit free travel only on those "rare exceptions where management judges that payment would be unfeasible and/or where consequent rejection of a trip would be fundamentally harmful to the *Post*'s news coverage or to its institutional public relations."

Dick Cheverton, news director of WOTC, Grand Rapids, Michigan, said acceptance of gifts was a matter of degree. "If the sum is very minor and refusal does not involve ethics but politeness, e.g., a news source buying a newsman a cup of coffee, the decision is one of judgment by the newsman," he explained.

At the *Los Angeles Times,* dinners, gifts, and favors for editorial staff members are discouraged, the paper reported. "However, we don't go to foolish extremes such as barring old friends from exchanging gifts because one happens to be a press agent," declared managing editor Frank Haven.

One reporter told *Quill:* "Seven years ago I toured a foreign country with a group of newsmen whose expenses were paid by that country. While I believe my reporting from that country was unaffected by the relationship, I also believe in retrospect that it was probably a mistake for my paper to send me on the trip and for me to accept the assignment."

Robert M. White, II, publisher of the Mexico (Mo.) *Ledger,* answered: "I find no Watergate of moral failure in a sports writer covering a game and taking a free seat in the press box."

Perhaps the most explicitly stated policy on staff favors is that of the *St. Petersburg* (Fla.) *Times.* Managing editor Robert J. Haiman laid it out in the Associated Press Managing Editors' *Guidelines* (1969):

All Christmas gifts of all kinds are returned with a note signed by the editor explaining our policy and asking that no future gifts be sent. Within just a year or two the packages of cheese, caviar, pens, paper dresses, etc., have dribbled off to nothing. The mail room has orders to deliver all such packages to the editor's office regardless to whom they are addressed. Since we don't let staffers get personal mail at the office, we can assume that any package coming to the paper is coming to the staffer in his professional status.

We accept no free tickets of any kind. This includes everything from the circus which comes through town each year to the local minor league ball game to the local tourist attractions. It's against policy for a staffer to get in any place with an admission charge on his press card and all such places in Florida have a letter from me saying so. When the sports editor takes his three kids to a minor league ball game on the editor's night off, he buys four tickets like any other father. The only exception we allow is that the sports reporter assigned to cover a ball game does not pay his way in and a reviewer assigned to a movie, play, ballet or concert does not pay. We scrutinized this carefully and see no conflict in accepting a ticket for the working reviewer writing that night.

We go on no junkets of any kind. The travel writer accepts no free plane tickets, meal tickets or complimentary rooms. If an airline is providing a free ride to inaugurate a new flight, we send them a check for the round-trip tourist fare if we go—which is almost never.

When we sent a man to Viet Nam to cover the war, we turned down the Pentagon's free press flight offer and flew Pan-Am. When we sent a man along with the gubernatorial candidates, the press planes were provided by the candidates. We sent them a check for the fares which would have been normally charged by scheduled carriers for the same mileage.

If we are going to a $100-a-plate fund-raising steak dinner for a politico and the reporter is going to eat, we send a check for whatever the restaurant or caterer normally charges for that steak dinner.

We accept no merchandise for "testing and evaluation." If the fashion editor wants a paper dress we buy it. If the food editor wants a rib roast, we buy it. If the golf writer wants to test some balls, we buy them. . . .

No one on the staff accepts anything from anyone for anything. No one on the staff owns anything or does anything which can gain him anything because of his job. And we pay our own way or we don't go.

A new policy prohibiting staff members from accepting complimentary tickets, dinners, junkets, favors, and so forth, has been ordered at the *Huntington* (W.Va.) *Herald-Advertiser,* as well as at other newspapers in the past two years. "As a business and as individuals, we pay our own way," said publisher N. X. Hayden.

The same idea was expressed by Thomas Winship, *Boston Globe* managing editor, when he ordered all staff members to no longer accept tickets or other freebies from teams and organizations. Winship said the new policy would enable the editorial department to avoid "even the appearance of influence." Tickets for working reporters covering games and other events are paid for by the *Globe.*

Outside Affiliations

The acceptance of gifts, free tickets, and other free-bies represents a rather clear-cut issue, which can be eliminated or limited by rules and edicts. Another conflict-of-interest problem is far more complex and presents a tougher decision on the part of media executives. The issue is simply this: Should news personnel be allowed to hold outside jobs in their communities or to maintain memberships and affiliations which could compromise their roles as reporters or editors? The query has produced no little soul-searching among newspapers and broadcasters.

At the outset, it should be stated that this kind of interest conflict often begins at the top. Liberal critics of the media are quite right when they say that newspaper and broadcast station owners are members of the Establishment in good standing. In scores of communities, local publishers and station proprietors belong to the country club, the Chamber of Commerce, Rotary, and other organizations whose ranks are normally made up of business and professional men. Whether such membership influences editorial decisions is an individual matter, but grounds for suspicion are present.

However, greater concern is expressed about the affiliations of reporters and editors since they have day-to-day responsibility for the news. Is it right for a newsman to hold membership in a political party? How about having an office in that party? At a time when the environment is a major story, should editorial staffers belong to environmental protection groups? What about being involved with the school board, PTA, civil rights associations, and the volunteer fire fighters? Traditionally, journalists have not been big joiners but some do have outside connections and insist on retaining this right. They claim their participation in these activities does not bias them. Further, they state that they should enjoy the same privileges in a free society as anyone else, be he doctor, baker, tool-maker, or insurance salesman.

The point is valid, but it fails to strike at the main issue. It is not solely a question of whether the reporter will be swayed by his associations but that the public may get this impression. In an era when the media are closely scrutinizing the ethical standards of public figures, publishers and broadcasters have become increasingly aware of the need to keep their own houses spotlessly clean. In keeping with this realization, the Associated Press Managing Editors Association conducted a nationwide poll in 1972 to determine the professional standards maintained by newspapers. Questionnaires were sent to 910 dailies, of which 229 replied. The survey indicated that newspapers had varying policies in regard to outside affiliations of their staffs, although virtually all the respondents did not let reporters work for competing newspapers.

Forty-one percent of the newspapers said they did not allow their reporters to hold political office, eleven percent "strongly disapproved," and thirty-two percent said they permitted it. Nine percent allowed reporters to hold appointed office and seven percent had no policy. Some newspapers said they even encouraged staffers to run for political office.

"Since the editorial policy of this paper is that every citizen has a duty to serve his country, we can't urge otherwise unless we are willing to participate ourselves," wrote R. B. Wellington, publisher of the Ottawa (Kan.) *Herald,* in his answer to the survey.

The *Louisville Courier-Journal* and the *Louisville Times,* which are owned by the same company, reported strict regulation of outside work by employees. Newsmen for the two dailies are not allowed to receive fees for appearances on radio or television within the newspapers' circulation areas. Neither are they permitted to work for a politician or perform any kind of publicity aid for an outside organization.

Perhaps the most flagrant example of conflict of interest was reported recently by the *Washington Star-*

News, which claimed that some forty U.S. journalists overseas were on the payroll of the Central Intelligence Agency (CIA). According to the newspaper's anonymous sources, most of the newsmen-spies were freelancers and part-time correspondents for American publications. But five were said to be full-time correspondents for major U.S. news organizations. Editors of the *Washington Post, The New York Times,* and other newspapers said they would quickly fire any reporter found to be in the CIA's employ. "It's absolutely not to be done," declared *Wall Street Journal* managing editor Fred Taylor.

A number of newspapers prohibit reporters from giving public relations assistance to political candidates and others—with or without pay. It would be embarrassing—if not unethical—for a newspaper staff member to be writing publicity releases for a candidate for a judgeship who was opposed by the newspaper. And if the paper supported the man, even more questions might be raised. Despite the crackdown on such practices in recent years, a few reporters still moonlight for political candidates without letting their editors know about it. In most instances, they face dismissal if they're caught.

The habit of moonlighting by newsmen and women is hard to stamp out completely because it's been around a long time. Compared to other professionals, reporters are not very well paid and can use the extra money. Also, politicians and others with a message to sell know that journalists are skilled communicators and have a sure instinct for what is newsworthy. In addition, reporters know how the media work, what deadlines are, and who the people are to contact on newspapers and broadcast stations. Besides all this, the politician figures that his material stands a good chance of getting into the reporter's own medium. He is willing to pay an attractive price for such services.

This relationship has led to some highly questionable activities by news personnel. A California reporter once managed the campaign of a candidate for the board of supervisors. In New York City, it was fairly common practice for the lower-paid reporters to engage in publicity work for political office-seekers. Newsmen also have written speeches and press releases for industry executives whose firms are frequently in the news. Certainly, a question is raised when a reporter in a steel company town turns out publicity material for a plant vice-president. Can that same reporter be trusted to write an objective story about the company's labor problems or a rise in the price of steel products? Perhaps he can, but suspicion is always present.

Some prominent editors and publishers also have flirted with politics in a way to draw comment within and without the news industry. Herbert Klein, President Nixon's former White House communications director, left his job as editor of the *San Diego Union* several times to work on Nixon campaigns. Pierre Salinger, press secretary to Presidents John F. Kennedy and Lyndon B. Johnson, took leaves of absences from the *San Francisco Chronicle* to labor for Democratic candidates before he met Kennedy. The late Philip Graham played a prominent role in the 1960 Democratic National Convention while serving as publisher of the *Washington Post*. Other newspaper publishers are actually delegates to the Republican and Democratic Presidential conventions. Writing in the July, 1971, issue of *Quill,* Richard Harwood, managing editor of the *Washington Post,* observed:

"Today there is desultory discussion among editors and reporters over the proper limits of 'involvement,' whether—in the fine phrase of J. R. Wiggins, former editor of this newspaper—one can 'reasonably ask the privilege of being on both sides of the footlights, actors on the stage and critics in the audience at the same time.' But there is ethical bankruptcy in the news business on that issue as on other conflict-of-interest questions. What is ethical on the *Daily Bugle* is unethical on the *Daily Clarinet*. There is even conflict and confusion within given newspapers."

Harwood offers a depressing view, but the picture is changing—for the better. The news media are taking a harder look at conflicts of interest and moving toward eliminating it. One reason for the change has been the heavy criticism leveled at the media in recent years. The Watergate revelations have been a factor, causing the media as well as many other institutions in this country to reexamine their codes of morality and conduct.

Freedom House, which researches American institutions, reported that the poor relations between the media and the federal government might be improved if both adopted a certain code of ethical practices. Following a conference on the subject at the University of Maryland, Freedom House proposed that journalists should be impartial and fair, should qualify the reliability of unidentified news sources, should protect the freedom of the press while respecting the rights of others, and should avoid conflicts of interest.

The conference also suggested that journalists should tell their employers of any outside income and should keep away from undisclosed activities that might raise questions about their objectivity in reporting news.

It was further recommended that government officials openly discuss what information they have and not withhold material for personal or political reasons. Additionally, they should tell newsmen when they believe certain disclosures will harm the country, and should not, without good reason, give out off-the-record information or provide false information. Moreover, the conference members said, all journalists should be given equal access to information.

Among those taking part in the conference were William Attwood, publisher of *Newsday;* Professor Alexander Bickel of the Yale Law School; Erwin D. Canham, editor in chief, *Christian Science Monitor;* Roscoe Drummond, Washington columnist; and Alan Jackson, CBS Radio News.

Conflicts of interest may also involve taking part in antiwar activities, social causes, and community welfare work. Is a newsman to be banned from such participation even though he believes strongly in it? The issue has been argued on both sides. Tom Wicker, columnist and associate editor of *The New York Times,* has spoken at antiwar rallies and defends his actions, explaining that he doesn't consider them political forums. He said further:

It seems, in most cases, that if you frequently attend the parties of political candidates, if in cases that I know about you have accepted rides in their airplanes to wherever you may be going for the weekend, that is not considered to be participation as such.

I think it is one of the most virulent forms of participation, and I would much prefer myself to be caught dead on the platform of an antiwar rally than riding free in the airplane of a political candidate. Also, a question has arisen whether the acceptance or taking of a position on a great public question—let's say the war in Vietnam or racial matters—leaves you subject to the discipline and pressures of factions.

Some people may allow themselves to come under the pressures and disciplines of political factions, but on the other hand there are a great many people who would not.

Geraldo Rivera, a reporter for WABC-TV in New York, was reprimanded by the station in 1972 for making partisan political speeches on behalf of the Presidential candidacy of Senator George McGovern. Al Primo, vice-president for news of the five stations owned and operated by the American Broadcasting Company, told *The New York Times* that ABC's policy prohibits newsmen "from taking sides on behalf of any one candidate or party."

William Sheehan, vice-president and director of TV news for ABC, said that he was "appalled" when he heard of Rivera's speeches for McGovern. "It's definitely contrary to all our policies governing behavior of news personnel," he added. "There are no gray areas in such cases; they're all black and white."

Following one of Rivera's appearances at a Mc-Govern rally, the candidate's publicity office released statements quoting the newscaster's statements praising McGovern and attacking the Nixon administration.

Rivera, an activist newsman, at first balked at ABC rules governing its reporters. "I've made no secret of my support for McGovern," he declared. "I intend to continue to visit universities and colleges to talk about social problems and I'll either answer questions about the campaign or volunteer my views on McGovern."

Later, however, ABC reported that Rivera agreed to follow company policy. It was either that or he would have been taken off the air, Primo said. Rivera, however, continues to include personal commentaries in his newscasts.

Black reporters for white newspapers and broadcast stations have found it difficult to divorce their jobs from their personal feelings about racial injustices in America. Many black newsmen experience a severe conflict from their efforts to be fair and even-handed while having little or no faith in doing so. As members of a minority group which has been subjected to discrimination, they feel obligated to give a black slant or perspective to news from the ghetto. Robert A. De-Leon, a black man who reported for *The Atlanta Constitution* and *Newsday,* recalled his newspaper days with a bitterness echoed by many of his black colleagues.

"Once involved in the black community," he said, "I found it increasingly difficult to remain in the position of objective observer and soon learned that such attempts were futile. I realized that my biases and subjectivity entered into the picture even before I began reporting a story. Because white papers—and the media in general—traditionally have neglected and, in fact, ignored the black community, editors provided little guidance in the selection of stories in the black community and the whole process of selection became a personal matter. I had to dismiss the notion of objectivity. In choosing stories I constantly found that I was seeking the *good things* that were being done in the black community. I guess I was trying to prove to whites that blacks were human and wanted, basically, to share in the same things as everyone else. For this bias I have never apologized, because white journalists have been doing it all along as it relates to the day-to-day happenings in the white community."

Betty Washington, a black reporter for the *Chicago Daily News,* said she strives for fairness in every story she covers, "even when I'm emotionally upset about something, like a police-Panther shootout." She admitted, however, that her story "is bound to be biased to a certain extent. I don't care, because I know how some other stories are written in the paper. Actually, I don't believe that anyone is objective. Newspapers certainly are not objective."

A former *Daily News* colleague of Miss Washington, L. F. Palmer, Jr., terms objectivity a "myth." He said frankly: "I believe in advocacy journalism, particularly for blacks. At the same time, I feel that a reader is in a better position to evaluate a story if the biases of the writer are not hidden. It's when they're concealed that the reader gets taken. If the reader knows that I am a pro-black writer, which I am, he can more competently deal with what I am saying." Mr. Palmer, a veteran newsman for both black and white papers, quit the *Chicago Daily News* to found his own black newspaper.

"I, as a black journalist, can no longer work for a white newspaper," he explained. "The objectives of the white press are at odds with the objectives of Lu Palmer. I could not carry out my mission."

Whatever blacks feel about objectivity, white newspaper editors insist on it for straight news stories. Advocacy journalism is still largely confined to the so-called underground press, certain black publications, and newspaper columns under the writer's by-line. Pete Hamill, Nicholas von Hoffman, Tom Wicker, and others manage to dish out a lot of opinion and take sides in their columns, which appear in scores of newspapers. Nowadays, too, several magazines have swung toward pro or con articles on a number of subjects, including health, welfare, politics, environment, crime, poverty, and so on. These include *Harper's*, the *Atlantic Monthly*, *The New York Times Magazine*, *Esquire*, the *New Republic*, *The Nation*, the *National Review*, and others.

Use of Names

The matter of ethics becomes somewhat clouded in other areas of journalism. For example, one public complaint concerns the use of names of juveniles arrested for crimes. Should a youth's name and address be carried in the paper or broadcast on the air if he is under sixteen? Under seventeen? Under eighteen? Most newspapers and broadcasters regard this question as a matter of policy, not ethics. The policy differs from paper to paper and station to station. Generally, names are not used in crime stories when the juvenile is under eighteen—unless the crime is a major one, such as murder. In a small town, particularly, it's almost impossible to keep names from getting out in a capital case. Concealment would also impose a burden on the newspaper or station to keep the name hidden all during the trial, which is hardly likely.

In minor drug arrests and misdemeanor crimes, the news media usually refrain from printing names, especially for first offenders. Juveniles also are protected in many states by having their cases heard in juvenile courts that are closed to the press and public.

Another editorial decision is whether to use the names of a criminal suspect's family in the story. Most readers and viewers would probably cry "unfair" at a news medium which, let's say, used the name of an innocent sixteen-year-old daughter in connection with an article about her father's arrest for narcotics dealing. Most news managers would agree and would not mention the girl if she played no part in the alleged crime. But the dilemma is not resolved as easily as all that. It's an old adage in the city room that names make news. What would an editor do if the daughter happened to be a famous movie actress, even though she had done nothing wrong? Many editors would, in this case, reveal her as the child of the suspect. Conversely, if the son of the president of General Motors is arrested, the father's name will most likely go into the story if the reporter has made the connection. Guiltless relatives, if they are prominent, may not like having their names in the paper or on the air but they are resigned to it. In our society, the price for being a celebrity or being rich is the attention of the media. A minor automobile accident will not generally be news unless one of the drivers or passengers happens to be well known. If the governor's limousine merely bumps fenders with another vehicle, the incident would excite an editor, even if no one was hurt.

What to Tell

Journalists are trained to be specific and include important details in their accounts. There may be times, however, when a news medium may give the public *too* many details. This can occur in crime stories which may contain a complete lesson on how to rob a bank, cut heroin, steal credit cards, or start an automobile without a key.

News executives are becoming increasingly aware of the possible harm such information can cause and step warily around such articles. Reporters, in fact, are often told to leave out certain things which might provide an education in lawbreaking. Frequently, this is a matter of cooperating with the police, who may ask newsmen to withhold certain material from what is published or aired. Nevertheless, newspapers and broadcast stations are still in the news business and don't like to hold back interesting details. News stories *have* contained fairly explicit accounts of how to embezzle money, counterfeit bills, steal and cash securities, make bombs, and illegally get on the welfare rolls. Citizens who deplore such reporting have a valid argument: Such information could give some people wrong ideas. However, it would not be reasonable to assume that there is a vast army of persons breathlessly waiting for the paper every morning so they can learn how to commit a crime. Crimes are generally committed by criminals who already know the techniques. Even so, newspapers and broadcasters have been cutting back in recent years on crime detail out of a sense of public responsibility. This action also comes at a time when the crime rate is on the upswing. The news media do not want part of the blame for the trend.

Identification of Sources

The reporter's use of such terms as a "White House source," "high administration official," or "State Department spokesman" may cause the media reader or viewer some anxiety or annoyance. Is the writer or broadcaster trying to pull a fast one? Why doesn't he name the person who gave the information? Why the secrecy?

In most instances, the newsman would be only too glad to reveal his source if he could. He is prevented from doing so because of the conditions under which he got the story. The "high administration official" would release the information *only* on a not-for-attribution basis. In other words, for one reason or another he does not want to be identified as the source. If the reporter demands to use the person's name, he is simply not given the story. On the other hand, if the newsman promises to keep the source's name secret, he is ethically bound to keep his word.

This is a tough decision. The reporter's job is to get the news. He would rather use the source's name because it makes the story more believable. But sometimes he has to compromise or walk off empty-handed.

Remember, he has competition. What if a rival reporter accepts the news on a non-attributable basis? The first reporter is then blamed by his editor for being scooped.

Instances have come up when newsmen have invented their anonymous sources. This is rare and risky. If a reporter is caught at this game he will be fired. Other journalists would hold him in the deepest contempt.

Official sources frequently will not let their names be used because their information is a "trial balloon." They want to test public reaction to a proposal or plan before they identify themselves with it. If the idea becomes popular, the source will step forward and claim credit. If it bombs, he may never reveal himself. These unnamed sources in Washington are frequently cabinet officers, White House aides, generals, and perhaps the President himself. The system also applies to state and local government and to the professions and industry. Quite often, the spokesman for such organizations as the American Medical Association or the "steel industry" may be a vice-president for public relations. These individuals are seldom identified in news accounts. However, the AMA source could be a doctor who feels that medical ethics would be compromised if he allowed his name to be used.

The not-for-attribution story is just one of the restrictions under which Washington and other governmental reporters work. There is, for example, the off-the-record comment. This means exactly what it says. The reporter accepts certain information with the understanding that it not be printed or any source mentioned. What good is such material? Not much, but the experienced reporter may find it useful as background for a story he someday will be able to publish. Also, it enables him to maintain his contact with the source, who next time will hopefully provide him with an on-the-record comment. In recent years, it has become fashionable for Washington officials to invite select groups of reporters to private homes or restaurants for "backgrounders." The practice has displeased the newsmen not invited and their editors. Then, too, there is the suspicion that the press is being used on these occasions as a conduit for new policies someone wants to try out on the public. However, some reporters feel that the backgrounder does increase their understanding of complex political situations. In any event, it would be unrealistic to expect political sources to put everything out in the open. The United States has· probably the most free press in the world, but we haven't yet arrived at that stage.

To sum up, ethical violations occur in various phases of the news operation, but standards have improved dramatically in the past twenty-five years and continue to do so. Both management and working reporters are becoming more aware of their responsibilities in a time when the media have been assailed, rightly or wrongly, for creating some of the evils in our society. Younger men and women entering the field of journalism are generally more idealistic than their predecessors of twenty-five to fifty years ago. They are also better educated and better trained, and many of them have a sense of mission—of contributing to a better world.

The media audience can aid in the development of even higher ethical standards by calling to the attention of the newsplant owners and managers examples of unethical conduct they may notice in print or on the air. As pointed out earlier, the media *are* responsive to public opinion.

CHAPTER NINE

The Media Watchers

PUBLIC CRITICISM OF newspapers carries little weight with editors. The attitude of a typical professional newsman is that the man on the street knows next to nothing about journalism and thus his opinions on the subject are without value. Some readers blow off steam in the letters-to-the-editor column but their missives are not known to influence editorial policy.

Broadcasters, as proprietors of a federally licensed medium, are much more sensitive to the waves of public opinion. Fifty or sixty letters to a station complaining about a program can produce a mood of worry and fright among executives. Expressions of discontent on the part of politicians concern them even more. The last thing wanted by the TV and radio industry is any more extensive government control over its operations. A speech by a vice-president or a congressman attacking some aspect of broadcasting sends shivers of fear through management.

In recent years, media criticism has come from another quarter: working journalists. The press and broadcasting are being examined by a number of magazines written and published by current or former newsmen and women. These publications include the *Columbia Journalism Review, (MORE)*, the *Chicago Journalism Review*, the *Southern California Journalism Review*, the *Montana Journalism Review*, and others. The basic idea of these magazines is to improve the press by focusing on its weaknesses. Writers come down hard on newspapers and broadcasters that kowtow to advertisers, accept favors from news sources, practice timid censorship, sidestep controversy, and generally avoid their responsibilities. For example, *(MORE)*, one of the more irreverent reviews, took CBS to task for dropping "instant analyses" of Presidential speeches. It also revealed the names of newspapers that had scissored-out certain "Doonsbury" comic strips because they assigned guilt to White House figures, including President Nixon, during the Watergate hearings.

The *Columbia Journalism Review,* published by the Columbia University Graduate School of Journalism, has assailed the white ownership of most black radio stations, cast a jaundiced eye on the quality of science writing in the mass media, and deplored coverage of various events. The *Chicago Journalism Review* has lambasted the Chicago newspapers for not having taken a stronger stand against the Chicago police department, whose members manhandled reporters and photographers during the 1968 Democratic National Convention. Journalism reviews feature constructive and praiseworthy articles on the media as well, giving credit where it is thought due. In this respect, the reviews compete with the more traditional magazines devoted to the media such as *Editor & Publisher, Broadcasting, Quill, Grassroots Editor,* and the communications sections of *Time, Newsweek,* and *Saturday Review/World.*

Journalism review writers and editors are generally young, idealistic, and, in some cases, embittered by their working experiences in the media. Some have left their jobs to free-lance or to go into some other field. Others write under their own by-lines for the reviews while continuing to hold their staff positions on newspapers, magazines, or broadcast stations. Editors may not like what these reporters say in the reviews, but there is little likelihood they will lose their

jobs over such moonlighting. Such action would be hard
to justify, even for the most vengeful editor. Judging
by some of the outraged responses to review articles
by editors and station managers, these publications are
closely read by the industry. There is reason to believe
that the criticism has provoked changes in various news
operations. When a *New York* Magazine article disclosed that many *New York Times* sports stories were
really submitted by public relations men, the managing
editor promised to halt such practice.

The journalism reviews may be an irritant to publishers and broadcasters, but they take second place to
another media watcher, the National News Council,
only a few weeks old at the time of this writing.

By its own description, the council is an "institution designed to serve the public by promoting accurate and fair reporting by the nation's press." Its main
function is to investigate public complaints against
national print and electronic media—the big wire
services; the national news chains, such as Newhouse,
Knight, and Gannett; national weekly news magazines;
broadcast networks; public television and radio; *The
New York Times* news service; and other syndicated
services.

The idea of a news or press council to act as a kind
of ombudsman for the public is not new. Such agencies
have long been established in England, Sweden, Fin-
land, and other countries. Nor is the concept new in
the United States.

In 1947, a commission headed by Robert M. Hutch-
ins, then Chancellor of the University of Chicago, issued a report, *A Free and Responsible Press*. It called
on the media to give a "truthful, comprehensive and
intelligent account of the day's events in a context
which gives them meaning" and to function as a "forum for the exchange of comment and criticism." The
commission members, who were mostly social scientists, philosophers, and lawyers (no journalists), also
recommended the establishment of an independent
agency to monitor the media on a day-to-day basis.

DIANA MARA HENRY

Marianne Means, columnist for the Hearst Newspapers, speaks on "Political Columnists: Can They Be Cosmic Three Days a Week?" at the 1973 Liebling II Conference. Named after the late A. J. Liebling, a well-known press critic, the meeting was called to take a critical look at news media performance.

Since that time, local or regional press councils, composed of lay citizens and publishers, have been set up in Bend, Oregon; Redwood City and Riverside, California; Cairo and Sparta, Illinois; Littleton, Colorado; and the state of Minnesota. Most of the local councils were created by a grant from the Mellett Fund for a Free and Responsible Press and are concerned only with local media. The councils had no power to force papers to make any changes. It could study, discuss or vote, always with the publisher as a member of the group. However, the council was not organized by the paper or station but by a university professor picked by the Mellett Fund.

Dr. William L. Rivers, Stanford University journalism professor, who helped organize the Bend and Redwood City councils, summed up his and his colleagues' experiences this way in the book *Back-Talk:*

First, it is important to point out that the media were not transformed by the councils. The newspapers and the radio and television stations remained pretty much what they were. Most of the changes were of degree, not kind—and many were by very few degrees. Anyone who expected a council to turn a small-city daily or weekly into a reasonably exact facsimile of *The New York Times* might say the councils had little effect. But we who conducted the experiments recognized limitations imposed by geography, economics and myriad other factors. Our goals were more modest, and we came away convinced the councils were a distinct success.

In the Bend and Redwood City councils, members raised the following general questions:

1. Does the press transmit its views and ignore others?
2. Is the press influenced by advertisers?
3. Does the press forsake the significant for the trivial?
4. Does the press resist social change?
5. Does the press invade privacy?

DIANA MARA HENRY

Marilyn Robinson of WRC-TV (left) and Ken Walker of the *Washington Star-News* field questions on a panel, "Is Anyone Covering the City of Washington?", at the 1973 Liebling II Conference.

More specifically, the councils sought and, in many cases, learned the answers to these questions:

1. Did the headline "How to Keep Unions Away from the Door" attack labor?
2. Why aren't trials covered as fully as arrests?
3. Can't papers summarize accident reports to give reporters more time for important stories?
4. Why aren't the papers hiring more black reporters?
5. Why must women have segregated news?
6. Why publish the names of juvenile offenders?
7. Why does the paper carry so many stories on plane crash victims?

In Littleton, Colorado, the establishment of a press council led to the inclusion of more youth news in the local paper. The Sparta and Cairo, Illinois, councils, which were composed of housewives, school officials, and business and professional people, were credited with making publishers more aware of the desires of citizens and of the need for responsible reporting. William H. Morgan, publisher of the Sparta *News-Plaindealer,* said: "The council certainly gave me a much better idea of what my readers notice and don't notice in the paper. We also know more now what the community expects from the newspaper and we've made some changes." One change was a more thorough coverage of city hall.

At the same time, the councils gave publishers and station managers the opportunity to explain how their enterprises are run—the difficulties of production problems and the like. Few people really understand the meaning of a deadline or how space is allocated in a newspaper.

"It gave publishers the chance to tell interested citizens why a newspaper operates as it does," Rivers said.

The Riverside Press Council reported mixed results in its monitoring the *Riverside Press and Daily Enterprise.* The eleven-member body found that the newspaper was "generally accurate" in its coverage of the Riverside Housing Authority but "seriously inaccurate" in its report of a Board of Supervisors meeting. The council also decided that the coverage of local clubs and organizations could stand expansion and improvement.

The Board of Supervisors meeting concerned a dispute over a proposed four-lane highway through Coyote Canyon in the Borego Desert. The council said the paper presented the positions of two supervisors as being for the highway when, in fact, they were against it. Publisher Howard W. Hays, Jr., admitted the account of the meeting had not been as accurate as it should have been.

"We regret this and are indebted to the council for bringing it to our attention," Hays added. "Since learning of it, we have reviewed the handling of the story with those on the staff who were involved in order to minimize the danger of repetition." He asserted that the story was "in no sense typical of our local news coverage nor the efforts of those responsible."

The Riverside Council had a simple procedure for handling public complaints about the newspaper. When a gripe came in, copies were distributed to all members so they would be prepared to discuss it at the regular monthly meeting. If the council decided a complaint merited investigation, the chairman assigned the matter to an ad hoc committee which gathered background and interviewed the principals in the case. The council did not consider complaints dealing with editorial policy or taste in news stories or photographs. Such letters were sent to the newspaper, however.

The Wilmington (Del.) News-Journal has no press council but it does have an ombudsman, who handles public complaints about the newspaper. Cy Liberman, who has the title of "Public Editor," also writes a column in which he explains for the reader such newsroom operations as editing. The newspaper also prints daily correction boxes of errors. Liberman, who has been given a free hand by management, said that he never argues with a disgruntled reader. He assures the person that the accuracy of the story in question will be checked out and, if found to be wrong, will be corrected in print. Liberman also deals with the complaints of staff members about errors in the press.

Local press councils and ombudsmen have been tolerated, even by publishers and broadcast owners who are not wildly enthusiastic about the idea. They know these agencies contribute to good public relations for the media as well as imparting a beneficial effect to editorial performance, namely accuracy and fair reporting.

The new National News Council, on the other hand, has run into serious opposition from the media. The list of newspapers and organizations opposed to the council reads like a Who's Who of journalism. The American Society of Newspaper Editors polled 740 members, and of the 405 who replied, three out of four opposed the idea of cooperating with the council or any other outside group. The prestigious *New York Times* has come out flatly against the council. In a memo to his staff, publisher Arthur Ochs Sulzberger announced that the newspaper had decided not to cooperate in any way with the council. The *New York Daily News* called the council a "sneak attempt at press regulation, a bid for a role as unofficial news censor. . . ."

Clayton Kirkpatrick, editor of the *Chicago Tribune,* said there was no need for a news council because "newspapers are better than ever. They have made good progress historically in closing the credibility gap." He added that he opposed press councils generally because they are "based on false premises" in assuming that there are universal standards of what is true, fair, and responsible. Such factors are not easily determined, he maintained.

In a scathing editorial, the *Los Angeles Times* expressed fear that the council, "however well motivated," will restrict the flow of information from an already intimidated press. The editorial declared further:

Although the proposed council addresses itself to national news media, it's hard to see how this could fail ultimately to include practically the entire press, since the output of wire services and other alliances comes from individual newspapers of all shapes and sizes.

OK. None can deny that the press is sometimes pretty bad, sometimes wrong, sometimes careless. For this it deserves criticism—and gets it. From public officials, from community figures, from readers, from every quarter.

If a group wants to establish itself as a more formal agent of critical judgment—leaving aside the important question of its qualifications—OK, too. But it does seem unreasonable to expect the press to join in. . . .

William Payette, president of the national journalism society, Sigma Delta Chi, termed the council "dangerous." *The Wall Street Journal* commented: "We do not require help from a self-appointed, quasi-public com-

mittee to do this job and to serve the public interest."
John S. Knight, publisher of the Knight Newspapers,
said that "any self-respecting editor who submits to
meddling by the council is simply eroding his own
freedoms."

The ABC and NBC networks have refused to cooperate with the National News Council, although CBS
has endorsed it. The *Arizona Republic* issued this
blistering attack:

Aside from the dangerous moral implications the council
has on First Amendment rights of the press to operate un-
fettered, the council is plainly in no position to judge nor
effectively control media performance. Responsible print
and electronic media have long been sensitive to their own
performance through reaction of viewers and readers. Electronic media are subject, for example, to relicensing and
fairness doctrines based on performance.

Newspapers have opened their letters-to-the-editor columns to enraged and outraged readers, and further ex-
tended their self-examination to readership studies and
the ups and downs of circulation. Citizens whose legal
rights are abused by the media have recourse in the courts.

If the track record of grievance groups in the past is any
measure, the council largely will be deluged with protests
which ultimately will involve the question of who judges
what is news and what is not news. . . . America has the
freest and most honest and most professional press any-
where in the world. . . . If there is anything the American
press doesn't need it is the so-called National News Council.

Undaunted by these brickbats, the council set up
shop in New York City in July, 1973, with William
B. Arthur, former editor of *Look* Magazine, as executive director. The council, which is sponsored by the
Twentieth Century Fund, is made up of nine public
members and six persons from the media.

The council considers two types of complaints: those
from any citizen or group in the U.S. concerning the
accuracy or fairness of news disseminated by national

news media; and media complaints from any news organization concerning attempts to restrict the freedom of a national news medium to gather and report news. The council does not involve itself in editorial comment. Complaints must be filed within ninety days of the date on which the questioned item was published. The complaint must state in writing the name and address of the person or organization filing it, the organization complained against, and the precise grounds and facts relating to the protest.

If the council's grievance committee decides to hear a complaint, it sends a copy of the accusation to the news organization cited with a request that it file a written reply within thirty days. If the two parties can settle the issue by themselves, the council takes no further action. If agreement is not possible, the committee will conduct an inquiry to determine whether the charge should be dismissed or a hearing held. If the latter is decided, both sides will be notified in writing. The council, however, has no power to force any party or witnesses to testify or provide information.

Following the hearing, the grievance committee makes its recommendation to the council by majority vote. If the council accepts the recommendation it issues a report, which will be made public.

At this writing, the National News Council has found some complaints justified and others without merit. The rationale of the council obviously is that media performance is more likely to improve if shortcomings are revealed by a responsible, impartial body. It is also obvious that this reasoning carries little or no weight with the newspapers and broadcast stations opposed to the council. They argue, and with some justification, that they are already under scrutiny by government, professional critics, readers and viewers, and special interest organizations, such as political parties, the American Medical Association, and the American Legion. Media people also are aware of the wave of public feeling against them that has developed in recent years and feel that news councils are likely to fan this hostility.

Not all the media community is opposed to the National News Council. Journalists who are members of the council include Ralph Otwell, *Chicago Sun-Times* managing editor; Loren Ghiglione, publisher of the Southbridge (Mass.) *Evening News;* and Molly Ivins, co-editor of the *Texas Observer.* The council's task force, which did the original planning, had such members as Barry Bingham, Sr., publisher of the *Louisville Courier-Journal;* Richard Harwood, a *Washington Post* editor; Louis Martin, vice-president and editor of the *Chicago Daily Defender;* Stimson Bullitt, King Broadcasting Co., Seattle; Richard Salant, president of CBS News; and John B. Oakes, *New York Times* editorial page editor. Oakes's service on the task force, however, was an individual decision and the *Times,* at this writing, is not doing business with the News Council.

Otwell gave the following explanation for his cooperation with the council and the reasons he felt a need for a media monitor:

Although credibility has been strained at times in our history, there was always a diversity of voices to permit nearly everyone to put his faith in at least one editor, one writer, one newspaper. And most of those who lost credibility also lost their readers, their advertisers and eventually their presses.

But now we've entered an age of bigger government, bigger problems, bigger divisions in society—and a bigger, more powerful press. And this leads me to what I think is the essence of the case that should be made for a national press council. Our credibility is sorely strained, and is undergoing new erosion all the time. . . .

It would be foolish for anyone to say that a press council is some kind of panacea in winning greater respect and trust—obviously there are other things which the press, or at least some segments, must do in addition.

But the value of a press council is in at least providing

an independent, hopefully detached, prestigious forum for hearing complaints.

It would represent an escape valve for those who have been frustrated in their efforts to be heard. As a complaint desk in the national department store of information, it would be there for all to see, and *some* to use.

News Council Director Arthur maintains that the organization was created because "media credibility has been diminishing steadily over a period of years, inviting a step-up of governmental attacks and encroachment on First Amendment rights." He declared that the public will benefit from the council's activities, and noted that, in addition to working for a more responsible press, the council will also investigate complaints against the government and the courts. Every complaint, he said, will be answered. "We owe it to the people."

It's too early at this point to say whether the News Council will live up to the hopes of its supporters. But it seems to be an idea whose time has come. If it works it could mean a new era in journalism which would see an improvement in media performance and a greater public respect for newspapers and broadcasters.

CHAPTER TEN

The Future of the News Media

CRYSTAL-BALL GAZING always involves hazard, but a peek into the future of the news media offers a reasonably clear view.

Today's developments make certain predictions fairly easy. Newspaper technology, for example, is bound to increase and eventually encompass most daily and weekly papers. This includes automation of the printing process and the use of electronic editing and writing equipment in the newsroom. Several papers already are completely or partially automated, and the trend is continuing. Printing unions, which for years resisted automation on the theory that it eliminated jobs, are now compromising with management in installing the devices. A particularly significant agreement on the issue was reached recently between the union and the two San Francisco newspapers.

The handwriting is on the wall. Production costs have become so high that a newspaper unwilling to invest in the new equipment runs the risk of going out of business. Several newspapers have folded since World War II largely because they could not meet their overhead. Automation does cost jobs, but negotiators for the unions and management can arrive at an equitable arrangement whereby the jobs are eliminated through attrition rather than wholesale firing.

The mechanization of newspapers will benefit the

public because more newspapers will survive. This enables readers to obtain their information from different newspapers, compare them, and reject one or the other. In short, there will be more than one voice.

Will automation produce more responsible newspapers? By itself, no. However, indications point to an increased sense of responsibility in both the broadcast and print media. This is a continuing trend, but the trend is being accelerated by criticism of the media by the government and the public. It's a safe bet that newspapers and broadcasters will get tougher about staff conflicts of interest, the accuracy of reporting, and fairness. It appears now that the Federal Communications Commission will take a more active role as a broadcast industry watchdog, thus putting station managers and news editors into a position where they must lean over backwards to avoid criticism. This is not, in the author's opinion, a healthy situation. If a democracy is to flourish, intimidation of the news media will not be a contributing factor. For technical reasons, TV and radio licensing will have to be continued. But it will be much better if broadcasters improve their own houses without government interference in the presentation of information. However, a hands-off policy is not likely to prevail in government-media relations. The growing mood of conservatism which has led to the election of a hard-line administration and a generally passive Congress shows little sign of changing.

News coverage is shifting in emphasis, a process that will probably accelerate in the next ten years. Readers and viewers will see more magazine-type journalism in which the news will be given more depth. Newspapers are almost forced into this change because television and radio are becoming the prime sources for spot news. The Watergate revelations brought home the value of investigative reporting and the lesson was not lost on newspaper editors. Investigative reporters will be sought after, paid more money, and be given more space. There also will be more analytical stories explaining our society, our problems, and our relations

M. L. Stein, formerly Chairman of the Department of Journalism and Mass Communication at New York University, instructs a student during a reporting class.

with other countries. Media specialists will increase in numbers.

To accomplish all this, journalists will be better trained. The journalism schools already have revamped their programs to produce a better educated and informed reporter. Tomorrow's media will belong to newsmen and women who can do more than play a typewriter. They will be journalists who have a keen understanding of the world in which they live. Many of them will be specialists because journalism is becoming more specialized. Look for more experts in the fields of medicine, race relations, science, politics, labor relations, environment, education, cultural affairs, and areas that have only begun to be cultivated as specialities in the media. Urban affairs is one example. J. Edward Murray, former president of the American Society of Newspaper Editors, said: "With increased education, newspaper readers have upgraded their expectations. They want better, more useful newspapers. And as modern life has become increasingly complex, so has the news and information which people need to cope with it."

Indications of another tendency were contained in this statement made by Larry Jinks, executive editor of the *Miami Herald* and Chairman of the Continuing Studies of the Associated Press Managing Editors Association: "Reporting is beginning to reflect the total community rather than only the so-called mainstream. We are gradually getting away from producing white middle-class papers for white middle-class readers. Ethnic and minority perspectives are finding their way into our newspapers, however imperfectly.

"More newspapers and more reporters are now oriented toward providing information that is useful to the reader, whether it is how to save money at a supermarket, how to teach your children about sex, or how to collect Medicare. This is not a new trend, but it is a rapidly accelerating one."

Newspaper editorial pages also will most likely undergo revision. Some dailies already are getting away from or modifying hard-line political stands. Instead, these publications are giving readers more background information to allow them to make more intelligent judgments of candidates on their own. The *Los Angeles Times,* for example, has virtually abandoned the traditional practice of endorsing political candidates and has taken its editorial cartoonist off the editorial page. In explaining its action, the *Times* said:

"With the development toward fewer and larger metropolitan newspapers came both a decline in partisanship and an increased effort by newspapers to look behind the daily flow of surface events to examine their cause and consequences. This attempt to put events into context is more useful to the readers than a mere account of daily events—in fact it is essential. It requires professionalism and good judgment and above all a sense of fairness. No newspaper without a strong sense of fairness can call itself great or even good."

Few newspapers have gone this far, but there is a fairly general movement away from dogmatic editorials in the old style of American journalism. Strong partisan feelings are giving way to a more balanced view—even on the editorial pages. There is a strong chance this idea will continue to expand.

Broadcasting will probably shift, also, to more specialized reporting on a more limited basis. There are no signs that news or public affairs programming will replace or even come up to the time-level of entertainment on television. One thing, however, seems certain. A current emphasis on professionalism will continue in broadcasting. Pretty faces and mellow voices are still being sought, but station news executives are looking mainly for trained, well-educated young people for their news staffs.

More "reporter power" also seems on the way. Reporters are demanding, and in several cases getting, a voice in the policies of their news organizations. This movement, which is already well established in Western European nations, notably West Germany and France, is catching on in the United States. Edwin Diamond, writing in the *Columbia Journalism Review* (Summer, 1970), remarked:

"Journalists who have followed the fight of parents to decentralize schools, the demands of students to have a say in the investment policies of universities, and the blacks' and radical whites' challenge to the established institutions of society, have now begun to think about applying to their own lives principles of community control, participatory democracy and collective action."

This application has taken some interesting forms which are gaining in momentum. Editorial staffers of the Gannett Newspapers are sitting in on editorial board meetings. On the Providence (R.I.) *Journal and Bulletin,* a committee of reporters has met several times with management on staffing and policy decisions. Newsroom employees at the Minneapolis *Tribune* also have made their views known to management, which acceded to some of the requests.

NEW YORK UNIVERSITY

Colleen Sullivan, a New York University journalism major, gets instructions from Tom Zumbo, UPI editor, during her internship at the press association.

The insistence on a stronger voice in policy is coming primarily from younger staff people. Many editors and publishers are willing to listen for fear that the complainants will seek jobs elsewhere. Besides, the managers realize that the young men and women often have good ideas to contribute. Investigative reporting, which has led to Pulitzer Prizes for some newspapers, has often been initiated by younger staffers. Newspapers and broadcast stations that want to stay in competition cannot afford to ignore junior workers. The day is likely to come when staff participation in policy-making is written into union or individual contracts.

Woman power is another development of which more will be heard. Women have long been unhappy with their status in the media. With few exceptions, women are second-class citizens in the news business. On newspapers they're found mostly in the women's section, although this is less true in the case of the suburban papers. A college-educated female trying to break into the broadcast industry is almost certain to be offered a job as a clerk or typist, with duties any well-trained high school girl could do. It's the same way in public relations. Of all the mass media, magazines offer the best opportunities for women casting their eyes on editorial jobs.

The women's liberation movement of the 1970s has made certain inroads into the news media. Protests by distaffers on *Newsweek* and other magazines opened up more writing assignments for women. This was just the first trickle of the waterfall. Women on newspapers, on magazines, and in broadcasting have shown they can compete successfully with men as reporters, writers, editors, and producers. As of this writing, Charlotte Curtis has been appointed editor of *The New York Times*'s prestigious Op-Ed Page, which carries editorial comment by staff members and outside contributors. The position had been held by a man, the renowned Harrison Salisbury, since its inception. Women are writing about politics, world affairs, science, and finance on the *Times* and other newspapers. Mary McGrory and

ABC

Marlene Sanders, now a documentary producer and writer for
WABC-TV, delivering a TV news report

Sylvia Porter are eminent columnists on politics and economics, respectively.

As the older generation of editors and publishers leaves the field, more women will assume responsible editorial jobs in the news media. This already is taking place in television, where solid, on-the-street reporting is done by newswomen on the networks and on local stations in New York, Chicago, San Francisco, and Cleveland. Marlene Sanders of ABC-TV was the first woman to anchor a news show and is now one of the few women producing documentaries.

Journalism school enrollment is almost 50 percent female now and the trend shows no signs of subsiding. In ten years, these women graduates will be filling half the news posts in the nation. So-called women's news itself will change more than it has already. The trend toward daily newspaper and magazine reporting of formerly taboo subjects such as abortion, birth control, sexual mores, drugs, etc., will continue and go beyond the bounds now set. The American public, notably

NEW YORK UNIVERSITY

Clive Barnes, drama and dance critic for *The New York Times,* teaches a class in critical writing at New York University's Department of Journalism.

women, have indicated a desire and a capacity to read and know more about these topics. Metropolitan newspapers and national magazines are now covering these issues routinely. The next step—and it will come—is for the community and small-town papers to report on these areas with greater frequency and candor.

The employment of blacks and other minority group members will increase in the news media. In proportion to their number in the total population, minority reporters and editors, especially the latter, are poorly represented on newspapers and broadcast stations. However, a number of publishers and broadcasters are seeking minority applicants in journalism schools and elsewhere. More blacks, Mexican-Americans, Puerto Ricans, and Chinese-Americans are studying journalism and they will occupy more newsroom chairs in the next ten years. In cities with large black populations, editors realize that black staffers are often the only reporters in a position to obtain significant news from the black community.

The economics of newspaper publishing appears headed in the direction of more group ownership. Independently owned dailies are finding it difficult to resist absorption by such giant chains as Gannett, Knight, Thompson, and others. On its face, this is not a satisfying drift. Single ownership of many newspapers can—and does—lend to a mass-produced effect. Instead of individuality, some group companies impose on their papers a common identity in makeup, type face, editorial opinion, syndicated columns, comic strips, and managerial control.

But the group-owned papers have learned one vital fact: how to survive in an industry in which overhead keeps mounting. Many smaller newspapers have sold out to chains because they could no longer afford to stay in business. On the other hand, most chain papers are showing a profit. For one thing, the large groups can make cheaper purchases of newsprint and, in some instances, own their own forests. Newsprint represents an enormous cost to any newspaper.

WASHINGTON POST

As the paper's ombudsman, *Washington Post* staff member Robert C. Maynard handles complaints from the public and writes a column on media performance.

The shift toward group ownership could produce numerous benefits for the public if these companies acquire and develop a deep sense of responsibility. With greater resources, the parent concerns can afford to give readers better newspapers. By spending more money for news, they can supply small-town papers with some of the features and news stories now available only to metropolitan dwellers. If properly motivated, the chain operators can provide for a diversity of opinion by running local and syndicated columnists of different political hues. All these things are possible if the owners permit them, as, indeed, already is happening to some extent in some group organizations.

Finally, one prediction that seems the safest of them all is that the demand for information will intensify. As the world grows more complex, the need for understanding becomes greater. Look for a proliferation of media—both print and electronic. News is a growth industry if there ever was one. This growth can lead to a new dawning for mankind. Only well-informed people can make decisions that will change their lives for the better.

Index